AF822670

HEALTH CARE ECONOMICS

Michael D. Brown, President

Julie -
All My Best
Michael D. Brown
4-10-10

# An Eye on Economic Survival In the 21st Century

Copyright © 2010 by Health Care Economics

Non-exclusive licensing rights granted to the
American Society of Ophthalmic Administrators
www.ASOA.org

Cynthia C. Rosso, Editor

All rights reserved. No part of this book may be reproduced or transmitted in any form or by any means, electronic or mechanical, including photocopying, recording, or by any information storage and retrieval system, without the written permission of the author, except where permitted by law.

This book is intended to assist ophthalmic practice employees in operating the practice. It does not constitute the offering of legal advice. The views discussed in the book are those of the author and do not necessarily reflect those of the publisher.

ISBN 978-1-929196-18-0

American Society of Ophthalmic Administrators is an affiliate of the American Society of Cataract and Refractive Surgery, 4000 Legato Road, Suite 700, Fairfax, Virginia 22033-4003, (703) 591-2220.

# Table of Contents

# Table of Contents

# Dedication

I dedicate this book to my wife and children for their undaunted support of my endeavors to work with physicians in the health care environment. They have never complained about the extensive travel, the work hours or the late night phone calls. They have understood my need and utmost desire to assist physicians with economic problems. For that, I share my love and my gratitude.

Michael D. Brown, President
Health Care Economics
11313 USA Parkway, Suite 138
Fishers, IN 46037
MichaelBrownHCE@att.net

# Foreword

Four years of medical school, one year of internship and three years of residency – yet **not a single day devoted to the business of medicine**. You know what I mean. In today's world, your practice cannot survive without the business information you need to minimize inevitable business mistakes.

Complex decisions, complex planning, short-range and long-range targets and goals, limited and decreasing resources that make you unable to offset increasing overhead are just the tip of the iceberg. Debt versus equity, long-range depreciation, fraud and abuse issues, sky-rocketing malpractice insurance costs, coding and reimbursement, silent PPOs, HMOs, RBRVS, CPT, ICD-9 "buy in" and "exit" strategies, consolidation, personnel, overhead – all of this to contend with **and yet we only want to practice medicine**.

Undoubtedly, if we do not understand the business of medicine, we will not be able to continue to practice medicine – a passion that has inspired us all to survive medical school, internship, residency training and going into practice. Whether a single physician practice, partnership, single specialty corporation, or a large multi-specialty practice, you must pay individual attention to the business of medicine. The rapid decline in reimbursement has led physicians to retire early, quit or sell out to avoid dealing with the business issues. **The days of having the luxury and capacity of making financial mistakes in medicine are over**.

The experience shared in this book by an individual who has seen it all is an invaluable resource. Reading and processing the information in this text will help physicians to make some of the right decisions or, perhaps more importantly, avoid making some of the wrong decisions. Over the decade I have known Mike Brown, his astute ability to evaluate, assess, and predict the direction of medicine has played a key role in the development and success of our group practice. This is particularly important at a time when failure is very possible and survival is the hope. Mr. Brown has been very generous to share his experiences and important business information with the physician community, and to present it in a manner that has extremely practical application to the business and survival of our practices.

*~ Dr. Stephen Powell*

# Introduction

Over the last twenty years, I have had the opportunity to work throughout this country, as well as overseas, with numerous health care providers of the highest quality and integrity. Over that period of time, I always wanted to develop an economic guide that fosters a better understanding of the critical economic principles of survival in today's health care environment.

This book is intended as a reference guide for medical professionals at any level to answer their many economic questions. Through my years of work with physicians and other health care professionals, I have developed numerous formulas that can be valuable tools for health care providers in a myriad of situations and issues.

Today's health care environment transcends the concerns of quality care into basic business principles that providers must follow not only to be successful, but to stay in business. This guide serves as a reference source for some of those principles. It is intended to assist you as you develop your business strategy, armed with a better understanding of economic issues for the upcoming decade and beyond.

I sincerely appreciate all the efforts of my staff at Health Care Economics, Inc. in compiling this book. A special thank-you goes as well to Dr. Stephen Powell in Morgantown, W. Va. for contributing the foreword to this book. He is, without question, one of the finest ophthalmologists and human beings in health care today. His intellect and business perspective are unmatched. It is an honor to call Dr. Powell not only a colleague, but also a friend.

I hope that you and your staff find this book to be a useful reference not only for the present, but also for years to come.

*~Michael D. Brown*

Chapter 1

# Overhead & Expense Management

*When looking at overhead and expense management, what are you really trying to accomplish and what truly is overhead?*

We spend much of our time in ophthalmology dealing with revenue enhancement issues and coding. Whether it is a refractive, optical, ambulatory surgery center or a clinic, we must consider issues of overhead and expense management.

This chapter examines operating budgets, or expense revenue analysis, as well as the key areas of overhead and ways to reduce it. The chapter will also cover such areas as bulk buying concepts to enable you to manage your optical business, ambulatory surgery center, refractive department, and clinical practice better and more cost effectively.

The primary reason for dealing with overhead management is very simple: control costs and see greater profits. There are only so many revenue enhancement techniques you can use in an ophthalmic location. However, there is only so much you can do with coding or pricing. Ambulatory Payment Classifications (APCs) for Ambulatory Surgery Centers (ASCs) and clinics, limit some of your approaches to revenue enhancement. With this in mind, you must focus on what it costs to do business.

When looking at overhead and expense management, what are you really trying to accomplish and what truly is overhead? Every day I'm asked, "Should my overhead be 30%, 40%, or 50%?" My typical response is, "It depends on a lot of factors." It is very easy for me to tell you that the typical overhead expenses should not exceed 48%. Does anyone believe that? No, because it depends on several factors.

Real estate is a key consideration that can affect where your overhead percentage falls. If your ophthalmology practice owns its building, then probably, with the rental payments, tax management and other issues, your overhead may be a little above the norm. Usually, real estate and rental are about 5% of your overhead. I have visited many practices where ophthalmologists own, but rent out space at 8- 10%,or even 12%, and try to stay within fair market, but they often increase the rent to cover their management and pass-through costs

Staffing is another consideration. Many believe staffing is the number one expense in an ophthalmic practice. Should staffing be 15%, 18% or 25% of your overhead? It depends greatly on the longevity of your staff, pensions, profit sharing and many other caveats. It is undesirable for an ophthalmic practice to spend 25 cents on the dollar for staff. The safer threshold is between 18 and 20%.

What if the majority of your staff members have been with you for a long time? Don't you typically see an increase in their salaries? The answer is yes, but is that bad? No, it's not. The biggest problem in ophthalmology today, as with most businesses, however, is turnover. So, it isn't always bad to spend more on staff salaries for those who have been loyal and stayed with you for an extended period of time. If a consultant tells you, " You know, 80% of your employees will be vested in three years or more and you're going to need to be ready to match their profit sharing or pension. Maybe you should consider getting rid of some of those people," you should think twice. The idea of good staff management is to maintain and pay loyal staff members. Training new staff members can often cost you more in the end than rewarding your loyal, long-standing employees Always try to maintain overhead for staffing at around 18-22% and consider all your options when looking at reducing that percentage.

If you run a practice, you should know every component of your overhead. Have you ever broken down the ambulatory surgery center, optical shop and clinic by categories? Doing so will give you a better understanding of your particular situation. You want to consider each one appropriately, realizing that an ambulatory surgery center usually runs about 32-35% overhead, optical shops run about 55-60%, and clinics run 48-52%. You need to measure each of the key components as separate entities, breaking down expenses by cost center. This way the optical shop or the clinic won't suffer if you can't make money in the ambulatory surgery center, for example. You need to manage expenses and income independently for each area. .

It is important to develop a budget, anticipating what you think you are going to spend. How much are you planning to spend on frames in the optical shop or how much on clinical supplies? You need to categorize and track these items across the board. Clearly define every dollar amount and every expectation by percentage. Start the process of budgeting by examining all the key issues, including owner or officer compensation (generally 25-30%). We will discuss owner compensation in more detail later in this chapter.

## Written Plan

A written plan is essential in terms of business plan development and actual budgeting. Ophthalmic practices that don't utilize accounting statements also don't get profit and loss statements, balance sheets or statements of revenue. They are clearly missing out. Every practice should get financial reports on a monthly basis, not quarterly or yearly. Practices that receive the financial statements but don't review or analyze them are also missing out. Unfortunately, in today's difficult economic times, we've seen drops in business, especially in refractive or more elective types of surgery and services. We must focus on the true expenses.

When income begins to drop a little, the first reaction is often to scrutinize staffing and consider cuts. However, such cuts could take a toll on the front office, back office, billing or technicians. This knee-jerk reaction may come in the name of better overhead management, but it may not be, and in fact, probably is not the right approach.

## Objectives

The first objective we are going to examine is cash flow impact. We are going to look at categories of overhead and how they impact the bottom line. An ophthalmologist asked me once, "My overhead is 70% and I'm drawing 25% for owner compensation, keeping 5% in the corporation. Is that bad?" I respond that it depends on the numbers and the expense quadrants in the practice. It may or may not be bad, depending on particular practice traits.

It intrigues me when two ophthalmologists compare notes about their practices, revealing that one has overhead at 70% and the other at 32% — and both feel they are at the right level. However, when you dissect the categories of overhead, you know what you want to analyze and change. For instance, what is your budget for owner compensation? Some say you should draw 23%-25% or up to 30%. Owner distribution and income distribution would determine your owner compensation level. For expense management to work in your practice, you must maximize profits and lower overhead. You need to review all your categories to truly get results.

## Financial Reporting

Let's talk about overhead in terms of what we are trying to manage in your expense categories. Financial reporting offers a compilation of the income and expense figures for a given period of time. We can do much more relative to overhead management and cash flow through good financial reporting and understanding "the numbers."

Revenue enhancement is not the only answer to greater profit! Diversification is another option. If you haven't opened an ambulatory surgery center, maybe you need to look into that possibility. Perhaps you need to consider adding an optical shop or bringing an optometrist into your practice. Bringing in another ophthalmologist with particular specialties or diversifications such as retina, cornea, oculoplastics, etc. could also be a possibility. There may be other options that would enhance the volume and array of services you currently offer your patients. Diversifying in these ways can often increase your revenue.

Team leaders at each of your locations, (i.e. your clinic, your ambulatory surgery center, or optical shop) should report to you on the cost of doing business in their area. What is the actual cost for buying contacts or frames, or supplying the surgery center? If business components did nothing more than get together and buy medical supplies together, the savings potential is enormous.

When your practice needs something, do you run down to the local convenience or office supply store and pick it up? When you think you need it immediately, do you sacrifice the cost for the convenience? Obviously, there may be some items that you need immediately and must purchase in this way. However, you are probably paying a much higher price than you would if you built up an inventory or used bulk-buying techniques.

Our company has developed a strategic alliance with a bulk-buying supplier called Healthcare Purchasing Resources. This alliance has helped our clients save around 12%, which may not seem large to you until you realize that an average ophthalmic practice could save around $30,000 per year. By investigating and implementing alternative buying options, a savings like that $30,000 could become owner compensation at the end of the year or be used in other ways.

All ophthalmologists should get regular financial reports, but many do not. You should be getting reports at least monthly with a breakdown of every category. In recent months, we have received calls from doctors who are seeing a drop in volume from 8-10% to even as much as 30%. Some refractive practices have dropped as much as 50% in volume over the last six months. Without some form of financial reporting on a regular basis, you cannot adequately track your trends in income and expenses.

When you receive your financial reports and balance sheets, do go through them with your administrator or office manager item by item each month? Do you have timely and appropriate management meetings? Again, ophthalmology has always been very fortuitous from a cash flow standpoint. Ophthalmology is perpetually ten years ahead of other specialties both in terms of business sense and profits. If you have statements and review overhead expenses and income regularly, you will be in a better position to more accurately manage your overhead.

## Debt Restructuring

Many doctors want to make $.25 -$.30 on the dollar for owner compensation. You need to examine your home budget and your vocational budget, and look at how your money is being spent. Debt service items are also important. Many think they should re-finance their building mortgage and look at their credit line. Examining fixed expenses can save often hundreds of dollars. When you consider the hundreds of dollars saved on a change from one point to a one-and-a-half point drop in interest rates, it is often beneficial to look at refinancing or restructuring your debt.

## Large Capital Expenditures

What are your expectations in terms of the future of your ophthalmic practice? Are you looking at better efficiency and cost savings? Are you expanding your lanes? Are you buying things you really need or things you would just want? Make sure you have the budget capability to support major capital expenditures and that they do something profitable for the practice. Many ophthalmologists buy corneal topographers or other expensive pieces of equipment for their practices and then are shocked at the debt they have incurred. Was the equipment necessary? It may be clinically efficacious, but it may not be from a reimbursement or profit standpoint.

## Ambulatory Payment Classifications

Ambulatory surgery centers are moving toward a reimbursement scheme called the Ambulatory Payment Classifications (APCs). These new payment classifications can really have an impact on your practice income of anywhere from 5-10%. You need to be aware of this, to categorize each CPT code and know the reimbursement levels. The Medicare category system is no longer going to apply if the Deficit Reduction Act of 2004 and the APCs are both activated. If so, the potential impact on your budgeting is dramatic, and you must be aware of the APCs and how they affect your particular situation.

## Yearly Budget

Do you prepare a yearly budget? If you do develop a budget, do you measure it from month to month comparing actual figures with budgeted figures? Every month you need to examine the budget and make those comparisons. Without a budget and a regular budget review, you have no strong financial policy and management. Monthly budget review not only helps you find problem areas before they have a major impact on your practice, but also allows you to identify trends and opportunities to positively impact your financial strategy.

Included at the end of this chapter is a sample operating budget for a fictitious ophthalmology group. You can see the suggested categories for this practice and the categories that are the most critical for you as an owner or administrator.

## Rent or Own

Look at the very first category of the budget example—rent. This is probably your biggest budget category. When examining your profit and loss balance sheets for the rent category, are you around 5% on a yearly basis? You could be higher if you're the owner of your building and using rent as a tax management tool. Or you may be sitting closer to 10%. Earmark balance sheets monthly if you were over budget based on 5%. There are a lot of factors that you need to consider when deciding whether to buy a building or continue to pay rent. You can't make appropriate decisions without looking at all the components of ownership and its impact to your monthly balance sheets and the yearly tax impact.

Utilities, which are separate from the rent category, are listed separately. If you consider electric bills, utilities could range to about 6-6.5%.

## Staff Salaries

Salaries are undoubtedly the biggest challenge for any medical practice. Staff salaries average 15-18% of your budget. Are you within these parameters? Do you think they are reasonable? When you weigh salaries in an ophthalmic practice, you have to examine COTs, COMTs, office management staff and optical shop staff. You might ask, of all of the practices out there, how many actually fall in the 15-18% range? The fact is that fewer than 10% hit that range. Is that bad? As I alluded to earlier, if you have staff with longevity and loyalty, it may not be a bad thing. Some physicians will do anything to get their staff salaries down to 17%, but that isn't always feasible or workable.

Your staff salaries could be 25% if you're generating more volume, more retained cash and higher owner compensation. What the owners should be getting plays into this equation. It doesn't matter if the staffing is at 25%, if you can compensate the owner at 28%.

Many doctors feel their number one problem in a struggling practice is staffing. In many cases, this is true when there are numerous full-time equivalents (FTEs) over what there should be. The average FTE is about 2.7 to 3.5 bodies for each doctor, but that is nothing more than a general rule and doesn't always apply. Nothing should be set in stone relative to staffing. If there is an ophthalmologist with a W-2 form of a million dollars verses one at $200,000, then there may not be a justification to cut salaries or staffing. There could be a very logical reason for the number of FTEs on staff.

Some practices lease employees. This can often be a problem because somebody outside the practice is managing the employee. Leasing companies charge between 12-15%, whereas your staff salaries are in the range of 18-25%. This may be an option you want to consider for other reasons, though, such as expense write-offs on your taxes.

Do you have salary parameters? You know a receptionist starts at a salary point, earns a certain mid-point and then reaches a peak level. Every category of staffing should have minimum, mid-point and maximum levels. When does the salary ever max out for an individual who started with you twenty years ago making $18,000? There has to be a ceiling for each position. Nothing is wrong with taking a look at options for staff people who may be above the parameters. You may want to consider telling them they may not have an automatic bonus this year and freeze their salary. This may mean going to merit reviews every two years or other options. Therefore, establish a ceiling you don't go beyond. If you do go beyond it, then everyone's parameters will have to change, in which case you won't be running your "business" effectively.

## Officer Compensation

Officer or owner compensation is an issue that is as large as a convention center. It is an issue if you're in a big group of three or more ophthalmologists under a productivity distribution model. Your owner compensation could be 10-14%. It could more if you're a higher producer. As an overall rule, for limited liability companies and sole proprietorships, you should expect an officer compensation level to be about 23-28%.

Again, in giving you a guidepost, bear in mind this is a benchmark only. Your owner compensation may vary depending on your particular situation.

## Cash Flow

Does your practice have an interest bearing account to hold float money, or do you deposit and hold money in a checking account? By putting "extra" cash into a money market or other interest-bearing account, you can transfer money in and out and gain interest on that money in the interim.

Corporations, even sole proprietorships, should try to maintain cash flow. There are obvious tax advantages to running the cash out of the corporation at year-end, but you have to manage your cash needs with that in mind. If you are buying equipment in November, you should have at least 10% of your income left in your bank account. Very simply, if you're a million dollar corporation in total revenue, you should maintain $100,000 in the corporation to buy equipment or to re-capitalize. Many practices don't do that.

Many practices have no funding. They bleed every dollar out to pay owner compensation, staffing or whatever. Then, when they want to buy equipment, or build an extra lane, or buy anything, they can't pay cash. They don't capitalize, they don't utilize the tax advantages, and they end up borrowing money. They have to get a credit line and the interest that goes along with it. Then the topographer they bought that costs $21,000 is now costing $52,000 because of the interest. So, I strongly suggest you leave at least 8-10% available for buying new equipment or enhancing your practice.

## Outside Services

Outside services will include professional fees you pay to professionals outside your practice who support you. The key here is that the percentage allocated for those services should not exceed 6%. If the services for your consultants are 6.1%, they should be let go. You need to put your professional advisors together and challenge them. Tell them your expectations. What do you want your accountant to do for you? What do you want your health care consultant to do for you? What do you want your attorney to do for you? What is the expense associated with each of these professional consultants? Is the cost reasonable for the services and time you expect?

## Overview

These suggestions given in the area of overhead and expense management should be merely a template for you to compare your own practice. Examine various areas of income and expense management and consider how you can make them more manageable.

Expense management techniques such as bulk buying can easily save you 1-1.5% a year. Is that significant money? If you can save 15% of that, you have just knocked down a percent and a half in the overall cost. To make this happen, you should offer an incentive to staff for realizing and managing a reduction in expenses. For instance, if you have an accounts receivable person who should be pulling in more of what's due, have you considered awarding a bonus for making collections? This can sometimes be a very simple and profitable approach to consider. If you want to cut optical expenses, consider offering your optician a bonus for reaching a certain level. If you want to cut the cost of front office supplies, put a budgetary cap on supplies and challenge the staff to maintain that reduction of expenses.

Examine restructuring any debt you may have and decrease the interest you are paying. If you can save one point on the debt service you are paying right now, you could average savings of $250 a month. This could potentially add up to $2,000-$3,000 for the year.

Assign cost center responsibility to your team leaders or supervisors for improved overhead management. Team leaders should be held responsible for not only expense management, but for net income as well. You need to have cost center responsibility and hold your professional team people accountable. Your accountant, attorney, financial advisor and health care consultant all have a responsibility to you. Tell them your expectations and put things in writing so you both know exactly what the demands and expectations are.

To summarize, overhead and expense management deserves a greater focus today than revenue. Overhead expenses are manageable by using a template as a guidepost. Encourage individual staff people to document expenses and hold them accountable. Every month you hold them accountable and reduce overhead and/or expenses, at the same time increasing revenue, you are putting money in your pocket.

# Sample Operating Budget

| Description | 2002 | 1st Qtr | 2nd Qtr | 3rd Qtr | 4th Qtr | 2003 | Percent |
|---|---|---|---|---|---|---|---|
| **Income** | | | | | | | |
| Prof. Fees Dr. #1 | 705,586 | 181,688 | 181,688 | 181,688 | 181,688 | 726,752 | 41% |
| Prof. Fees Dr. #2 | 511,725 | 134,328 | 134,328 | 134,328 | 134,328 | 537,312 | 31% |
| Optical Fees Dr. #1 | 247,582 | 63,752 | 63,752 | 63,752 | 63,752 | 255,008 | 15% |
| Optical Fees Dr. #2 | 225,724 | 59,253 | 59,253 | 59,253 | 59,253 | 237,012 | 13% |
| **Total Revenue** | **1,690,617** | **439,021** | **439,021** | **439,021** | **439,021** | **1,756,084** | **100%** |
| | | | | | | | |
| **Expenses** | | | | | | | |
| Medical Salaries | 253,695 | 69,000 | 69,000 | 69,000 | 69,000 | 276,000 | 23% |
| Optical Salaries | 71,374 | 21,900 | 21,900 | 21,900 | 21,900 | 87,600 | 7% |
| Payroll Taxes | 54,895 | 14,589 | 17,812 | 11,482 | 12,646 | 56,529 | 5% |
| Health Insurance | 29,554 | 8,400 | 8,400 | 8,400 | 8,400 | 33,600 | 3% |
| Employee Benefits | 1,012 | 266 | 266 | 266 | 266 | 1,064 | .09% |
| Retirement Plan | 10,312 | 3,000 | 3,000 | 3,000 | 3,000 | 12,000 | 1% |
| Business Insurance | 20,723 | 5,440 | 5,440 | 5,440 | 5,440 | 21,760 | 2% |
| Clinical Supplies | 17,236 | 4,524 | 4,524 | 4,524 | 4,524 | 18,096 | 1% |
| Contact Lenses | 54,327 | 14,261 | 14,261 | 14,261 | 14,261 | 57,044 | 5% |
| Optical Supplies | 220,919 | 57,991 | 57,991 | 57,991 | 57,991 | 231,964 | 19% |
| Patient Relations | 134 | 35 | 35 | 35 | 35 | 140 | .001% |
| Office Supplies | 50,629 | 13,290 | 13,290 | 13,290 | 13,290 | 53,160 | 4% |
| Outside Services | 59,374 | 1,500 | 1,500 | 1,500 | 1,500 | 6,000 | .5% |
| Promotion | 1,777 | 466 | 466 | 466 | 466 | 1,864 | .2% |
| Professional Fees | 41,799 | 21,200 | 19,400 | 15,300 | 14,800 | 70,700 | 6% |
| Meetings, Dues, Journals | 9,176 | 1,200 | 1,200 | 1,200 | 1,200 | 4,800 | .4% |
| Rent | 175,953 | 34,800 | 34,800 | 34,800 | 34,800 | 139,200 | 11% |
| Leased Equipment | 2,183 | 1,500 | 1,500 | 1,500 | 1,500 | 6,000 | .5% |
| Repairs & Maintenance | 16,003 | 4,500 | 4,500 | 4,500 | 4,500 | 18,000 | 1% |
| Telephone | 14,451 | 3,793 | 3,793 | 3,793 | 3,793 | 15,172 | 1% |
| Utilities | 4,750 | 4,500 | 4,500 | 4,500 | 4,500 | 18,000 | 1% |
| Donations | 440 | - | - | - | - | - | - |
| Property Taxes | 10,032 | - | 5,100 | - | 5,100 | 10,200 | .8% |
| Depreciation | 87,688 | 15,700 | 15,700 | 15,700 | 15,700 | 62,800 | 5% |
| Interest | 8,602 | 4,400 | 8,300 | 3,800 | 3,600 | 20,100 | 2% |
| Income Taxes | 302 | - | - | - | - | - | - |
| Other | - | - | - | - | - | - | - |
| Interest and other income | (4,614) | (1,211) | (1,211) | (1,211) | (1,211) | (4,844) | |
| **Total Expenses** | **1,212,726** | **305,044** | **315,467** | **295,437** | **301,001** | **1,216,949** | **100%** |
| | | | | | | | |
| Income Before Physician Compensation | 477,891 | 133,977 | 123,554 | 143,584 | 138,020 | 539,135 | |
| Salaries—Dr. #1 | 303,180 | 30,000 | 62,800 | 57,760 | 106,800 | 257,360 | |
| Retirement—Dr. #1 | 30,000 | 6,125 | 6,125 | 6,125 | 6,125 | 24,500 | |
| Other—Dr. #1 | 8,778 | 3,672 | 3,672 | 3,672 | 3,672 | 14,688 | |
| Salaries—Dr. #2 | 141,403 | 30,000 | 48,475 | 44,515 | 75,750 | 198,740 | |
| Retirement—Dr. #2 | 30,000 | 6,125 | 6,125 | 6,125 | 6,125 | 24,500 | |
| Other—Dr. #2 | 4,884 | 2,600 | 2,600 | 2,600 | 2,600 | 10,400 | |
| Physician Compensation | 518,245 | 78,522 | 129,797 | 120,797 | 201,072 | 530,188 | |
| **Net Income** | **(40,354)** | **55,455** | **(6,243)** | **22,787** | **(63,052)** | **8,947** | |

Chapter 2

# Accounts Receivable Management

*With the shifting of reimbursement, it is becoming increasingly important to collect from patients. You have to consider that if you wait 60 days, you are only going to collect approximately 80% of your money. When you wait 90 days, you're only going to collect about 70% of your money. The longer the time, the more you lose.*

Accounts receivable and collections typically have been fairly reliable in ophthalmology. Because of changes in reimbursement as well as other factors, you need to be more cognizant of collections, both upfront and from third parties. Typically, our firm sees one month's activity in accounts receivable for most specialties; however, in ophthalmology we are sometimes flabbergasted by the amount of money carried in accounts receivable and collections.

Often, doctors create accounts receivable problems by having a "big heart," allowing patients extended periods in which to pay. Many ophthalmology practices have four-, five- and six-month backlogs in accounts receivable. They carry accounts that have been in some form of collection, but these are not truly accounts receivable. Accounts receivables are the accounts you <u>can</u> collect. When a doctor allows lenient payment policies to permeate the practice—stating to patients, "We'll get the money from you when you can afford it," or sending statements out without strong wording to encourage payment—it only fosters trouble for accounts receivables. It is preferable to set a timetable for payments, such as a particular amount in 0-30 days, another amount in 31-60 days, and so on.

Frequently, doctors think that the patient who doesn't want to pay will not pay. Maybe it's something that the practice would write off anyway. Often, when patients challenge fees, doctors back off because they fear that patients who start questioning money have other motivations that may very well lead to legal action of some kind. Some people will challenge you about fees, your fee structure and your correlating deductibles. Often, however, these are just intelligent people merely wanting clarification.

Accounts receivable and collections are basically educational problems. It is well known that the more you can educate your patients up front, the better off you will be in terms of collections. Some ophthalmologists are so kind-hearted that if the patient creates a sad scenario, they let the patient leave without paying the bill. You probably know the patients who won't pay when they enter your office. You still see them, and they are still dealt with in a professional manner…they just don't pay their bills. In court case after court case, rulings have favored the patient because the doctor didn't attempt to collect any money from them. It shows that in essence, the doctor wasn't interested in the service being sold (if you will) and didn't attempt to collect for it.

With the shifting of reimbursement, it is becoming increasingly important to collect from patients. You have to consider that if you wait 60 days, you are only going to collect approximately 80% of your money. When you wait 90 days, you're only going to collect about 70% of your money. The longer time passes, the more you lose.

Once you have a bad debt that you send to a collector, it is no longer part of your accounts receivable. So, in fact, if overdue payments fall into the 90-120 day category, they should never exceed 5% of your true accounts receivable. Any more than that is far in excess of the marketplace rate for service corporations. Average accounts receivable in the U.S., per a *Medical Economics* study, approximates that accounts receivable will hover around the 93-95th day of payment cycles. If you are generating $10,000 in charges per month and you are at 93-95 days, then you should have an accounts receivable of $31,000–$32,000. You can compute your own accounts receivable. Many practices are starting incentive bonus programs, which I will cover below. A collections incentive bonus program should not be a replacement for merit and productivity. You also don't want the collection incentive to be so aggressive that patients are offended. Here is where patient education is the key to improving your accounts receivable—through clear policies, informative brochures, and knowing your patients and their demographic make-up. If patients are entitled to free care, give them free care, but if you are writing off over 5% per month, you are going beyond the norm for write-offs. This issue is both a state of the mind and a state of the pocketbook, and it is going to become very important.

Our firm studied the accounts receivable procedures for several practices. We asked them such questions as: "If you maintain 25% of your accounts receivable in 0-30 days, is that acceptable and normal? If you have 50% of your accounts receivable in 30-60 days, 20% in 60-90 and only 5% in 90-120, can you deal with that?" They said yes to both questions, but you should think about not only your dollar value in accounts receivable, but also how much is in what area. Many practices post signs indicating MasterCard and Visa are accepted and that payment is due when services are rendered. Then on their day sheets or in their automated system, we found that fewer than 5% of patients actually paid something that day. This is not an insurance discussion; therefore we are not going to cover par/non-par Medicare (see Chapter 10). You must receive some type of payment from at least 75% of your patients per day in order to stay within acceptable norms. You have to both make some contact and receive some money.

A lack of financial policies usually is the root of many collection problems. Do you have good financial policies that are documented and followed daily by the ophthalmologists in your practice? When you have a MasterCard or Visa payment option available, but you still don't collect your payment, do you have a policy to deal with that? If a patient complains to your ophthalmologist about the cost, do you have a policy to handle that? When do you send an unpaid statement to a collection agency? When do you consult with an attorney? If you use a collections agency, they may make one call or send one letter and get paid for their services whether they collect the payment or not, which can be frustrating. Or, an attorney may send a letter and collect the full amount, but then you receive only 50% of it and the attorney keeps the rest.

Accounts receivable should also be broken down by insurance, so you can track what the third parties are doing. Through your software system, you need to be able to track the age of each account. Once the patient makes a payment and you submit a claim, what happens to the account? You should be following through. Money is money is money. If you wait six to eight months, your money will be worth nothing. Many ophthalmology practices realize about a 4–5% profitability line on net income. But, if you hit the 80$^{th}$ percentile, you will not be able to cover your overhead. You may be running more than 5– 6% of profitability, but once you hit that 60 days, you are in trouble. You've already lost, you can't pay your overhead, and you are in the hole. Secondarily, accounts receivable from patients should also be tracked. Which one of these should come first? In other words, would you allow the amount owed to grow larger with patients or with insurance companies? At what point do you say the responsibility lies with your patients?

We suggest you delay no more than 60 days with insurance and 90 days with patients. Some will disagree, saying they legitimately cannot collect all the money from insurance companies. Among the ophthalmologists our firm serves, we found that 78% of their dollars are third-party related, which leaves patient-pay at approximately 22%. Up to now in this chapter, we have dealt with the 78%, now we will deal with the remaining 22%.

## Demographic Information for Patient Tracking

It is absolutely imperative that complete patient demographic information be obtained when the patient is initially seen and kept current throughout the course of treatment. Information regarding relatives or friends not residing with the patient to contact in case of an emergency is also a requirement on patient intake forms. Information regarding credit history is also becoming standard. This type of information can be extremely helpful when tracking a patient who has moved or changed jobs without notifying your office. However, if the patient presents himself or herself needing emergency treatment, such as in a hospital or outpatient facility, you cannot legally demand proof of ability to make payment before administering care without abandoning a patient.

## Authorizing Courtesy Charges

Anytime you change the amount billed for a similar service to an insurance carrier, it adversely affects your fee profile with that carrier. You maintain a uniform fee write-off if the amount to which you want to reduce the charges after payment has been received from a carrier. What percentage of your practice should be considered courtesy charges for services? Likely your practice has treated nurses or friends, but how much of your charges per month should be in a courtesy mode? The standard to follow for courtesy charges is to keep them under 3%. Anything over 3% means your doctor does not have a good policy in place and is too easily swayed toward courtesy.

## Estate Billing

When a patient expires under your care, do you bill the insurance only and not the estate? What seems to be a generous gesture on behalf of the physician is often misconstrued as an admission of improper care being administered. Also, if the patient is never billed for the co-pay responsibility, the insurance carrier can demand reimbursement on the premise that the charges for services were less than the amount submitted. You should always bill the estate.

## Abandonment

Are you at risk of patient dumping (also called abandonment) when discharging a patient for non-payment of the bill? Patients have successfully filed abandonment suits against physicians who have refused them treatment because of a bad debt. You can, in non-emergency situations, demand cash payment of the past due account as well as cash payment for all future services before rendering additional care.

## Truth-in-Lending Laws

Any balance that requires more than four payments is subject to Truth-in-Lending Laws and must have the language associated with it. If you are not charging interest or a service fee, you must have a signed, dated agreement regarding the amount and frequency of payments that are expected. You should understand what constitutes truth in lending and what statements you must have on your statements to deal with that situation.

## Collection Costs

The patient is responsible for collection costs if advised when he or she is brought into the practice. This is an absolute requirement of the Truth-in-Lending Laws. As long as a patient is initially advised in writing as to responsibility for collection costs, you may add your collection expenses, court fees and collection agency fees to the account balance when it is filed for action.

## Accounts Receivable Policies

All policies relative to accounts receivables should be written down. The policies should be clear to everybody in the practice from the front desk to the back office. Practices have been too focused on putting collection and adjustment decision pressures on front office people. Every employee in the practice, including physicians, needs to be aware of the practice's collection policies so that there are no mixed messages given to patients. It isn't that difficult. You start the educational process before patients walk in the door with no checkbook, their mind made up, and they are hurting. You need to start when they call for the appointment. Education starts on the phone. If you say you are going to do something, then do it

## Bonuses and Incentives

Many practices could benefit from a bonus or incentive program for an individual or group based on accounts receivable and collections. For many groups, bonus or incentive plans can be staff motivators. However, some employees will cross the line, ignoring their normal job responsibilities, and abuse the opportunity. They mistakenly put all their energy into trying to collect every penny because of the financial reward. To stem off this potentially wasteful use of time, you may want to challenge them to protect the bottom line, which encompasses charges, collections, overhead and net income. Not every practice does this, but it is another way to push for better collections and lower accounts receivable.

## The Collector

When selecting the person to handle collection calls in your office, you must be careful. While he or she is working on the phone in the evening, there are certain laws that must be followed. You want to be sure also that your collector is credible and kind. A firm understanding of your policies is imperative. If you take time on the front end to educate him or her on what you truly want done, your results will be much better. Many people are dumped into accounts receivable management collections from entry-level positions, or they may be the newest person on the staff. The receptionist at the front desk also deserves credit for hard work done to promote collections.

## Effectiveness of Policy

Complete and accurate demographic and credit information obtained at the patient intake process, combined with the presentation of collection policies, facilitates maximum collection of accounts receivables. Do you have written financial policies for your practice? Do you have definitive, written policies that you follow? If you do, I commend you. Anyone who doesn't will have problems. It is extremely important to have strong communication and support for your office policy.

The physician must develop a clear practice policy regarding payment expectations with overt support of the policy. Notice the word overt, not covert. If patients ask about bills, refer them to the staff collections specialist instead of trying to resolve issues in the lane. Also, do not discuss financial situations while strolling down the hall or tell patients not to worry about a fee for service on their current account. Just leave it to the collection staff to do their job without interference. Do not decide ad hoc to change credit policies or lower your fee. Stay consistent.

Review your policy periodically. Up front, you need to have a financial policy and abide by it. It is recommended that you review your policy at least bi-annually for applications and for strategic changes in the market place. Make sure your policy is consistent with the philosophy of the practice and that the collection staff is following it.

## Staff Support

Keep in mind that your staff is implementing *your* policies. Never intervene in a way that does not serve your patients. Listen to staff suggestions and openly discuss them. You must have a clear understanding of the collection policies, and your staff has to respect payment expectations. Policies may be printed in the employee handbook as well as a procedural manual to ensure all employees are well informed. Every practice should have an employee handbook that includes this information.

When patients have billing questions, refer them to the billing staff or department. Do not answer the question without proper authority. Never allow patients to believe that they are not responsible for payment of their bill, and if you have information regarding a patient's ability, inability or intent to not pay a bill, inform the billing staff.

## Patient Orientation

Post a sign clearly stating that payment is expected at the time of service. You need to do this and mean it. You also need patient brochures and collection education. They must be very visible and not surrounded by other materials. Be sure all staff members are enforcing the placement of these materials. Clearly outline payment policy in a patient orientation brochure and incorporate payment expectations into the registration form. State your financial expectations when the appointment is scheduled or confirmed. Clearly state that payment is expected at the time service is rendered. Tell the patient what the expected charge will be, even if it's a range of charge, and that payment is accepted in the form of cash, check or credit card. Advise patients their insurance will be billed so they will receive direct reimbursement if the payment is applicable (if that is your policy).

Disclosure letters are an excellent way to get up-to-date financial information from patients. There are some who can't afford to pay you. Some doctors are not concerned about those people, and if they want to render the care, that's perfectly fine. It's the people that "stiff" the doctors that that are the problem. Some patients will see a luxury car in the parking lot and ask, "Why do you charge $67 for a full eye exam when I can go to the OD down the hall and pay only $45?" This type of patient needs you to discuss and show your disclosure statements and your brochures and other educational tools. It may seem embarrassing to you to send letters in advance of surgery asking a patient to sign disclosure statements, but it helps you avoid potential legal risk with patients who repeatedly do not pay you.

## Patient Check-in

At patient check-in, as noted above, state that payment is expected before leaving the office. If patients have an unpaid balance, remind them of the amount due and request payment by cash, check or credit card. If they want to pay at the time of check-out, note this on the charge ticket. Then, at check-out time you should clearly state the total amount due. A suggested wording is: ***"The charge today is $_______. Will you be paying by cash, check or credit card?"*** Do not offer the option of payment delay for any reason. Do not ask, "What do you want to pay today?" You merely ask them what form of payment they will be using.

Don't hesitate to accept a post-dated check, but if you do this, be sure the patient's receipt is marked unpaid until the check clears. If the patient refuses to make payment, provide a colored envelope with a notation of the charge, patient name or account number, date of service, and expected payment date. You should then follow on with a statement similar to, ***"No money? How much do you have with you today? We can accept $10, $15, etc. as a good faith payment."*** If they don't have a checkbook, you might say, ***"We'll be happy to accept your credit card or can we provide you with a counter check from your bank?*** (if applicable)." Or perhaps, ***"We are here until 5:00 to accept your payment today if you would like to bring it back."***

A patient says, "I will pay you after the insurance company makes payment." How many times have we heard that phrase? Your best answer is, ***"By paying your deductible now, you will assist us in keeping our operating costs at a minimum, which decreases the need to increase the fees in the future."*** Do you see where this is going? You try to have a planned response for each of their excuses in order to make it more difficult to avoid payment.

If a patient promises a later payment, make note of the promised date on the calendar within the patient's view. If the payment is not received by this promised date you need to notify the collection staff for intervention. If the patient suggests that the charge exceeded the service provided, make a very polite request to clarify specifically what the patient was unhappy about and respond immediately. When patients start challenging you on fees, you may have other problems beyond merely collecting the bill.

Make sure you ask your patient at check-in for any change in demographics, and record the necessary changes. Verify that no family members have had name changes. Also confirm residence, telephone, employment and change of insurance information (in terms of verifying coverage), and make a copy of the insurance card. This is nothing new to you, but overlooking details like these can wreak havoc with your accounts receivable/ collection efforts later on.

Make sure patients know they will be responsible for collection costs, by obtaining written acknowledgment of this responsibility with their initial registration. Annually, review the written acknowledgment with benefit assignment, if applicable, and verification of patient demographics. Provide a verbal and written reminder of cost responsibility and collection notifications, especially the final notification.

Recognize bad risk patients, the chronic debtors who always owe everyone. Once you find somebody who doesn't pay you, you will likely find they don't pay anyone else. Then you hire an agency that hopefully has the knowledge and ability to do two things: 1) follow the federal laws of collections (you need to make sure your agency knows these laws and abides by them), and 2) tithe the accounts. The goal is to avoid spending time in small claims court, so decide your own policies in your geographic area relative to your philosophy.

Chronic debtors are often complainers who will use any reason to not pay the bill. They are extremely clever people who know how to do that. They know when to complain, they will abuse everybody in the health care system, including you.

## Patient Registration Form—Insurance Authorization

You need to have an insurance authorization form. This can be something as simple as:

> *I hereby authorize John Doe, MD to release information acquired during the course of my examination and treatment to my insurance carrier as necessary to secure payment for any benefits due me. I hereby assign payment of said benefits to Dr. Doe for any medical procedures performed. I understand that I am responsible for all charges, regardless of insurance status, as well as any associated costs for collections, should such action become necessary. I agree that this authorization shall be valid until rescinded in writing or replaced by another agreement at a later date. A photocopy of this assignment will be considered as valid as the original. I have read the above and fully understand the terms.*

## Delay or Evasion Tactics

Patients who say, "The check is in the mail," or "I did not plan to get sick," are delayers. They are usually irresponsible patients who let insurance policies lapse or have no dependent coverage. People who change jobs or residences frequently are often a risk. You can observe these factors and track them to better understand how to deal with such people. Rarely does a patient bring up expenses, money or finances to the doctor. They come out to the front desk to raise the issue. When your patients are sick, they'll spend anything to feel better. When they are feeling pretty good, you rank below the electric bill on their priority list. With patient education you can change that.

## Collection Tips

As mentioned earlier, when you ask for cash, check or credit card, the patient has a harder time avoiding the issue. Whatever you decide: cash, check, credit cards, colored envelopes addressed to the office or post dated checks, where legal, learn the great art of negotiation. Put your most experienced person on staff in the reception/collection area. It is extremely important that the person in this position can handle the demands.

You education brochures should explain the Medicare program in very straightforward terms so that the patient understands that Medicare only pays at the 75th percentile. These should be brochures the patient will read and take with them. They should include your phone number and an explanation of fees, a gesture that patients will appreciate. Often, angry patients are upset because no one took time with them to educate them and explain things. With well educated patients, you may have 2-3% in bad debt, but usually not a large volume. Many of the geriatric patients don't understand their Medicare or any add-on policies they might have. They need everything explained to them thoroughly.

## Responses for Non-payment Excuses

***I forgot my checkbook.***

Give the patient a colored envelope with the amount owed.

***I still have the same problem.***

Remind the patient no promise of cure was made and the quality of care provided was delivered with the most current knowledge available for the problem.

***I do not feel I received the proper treatment.***

Here is a red flag. Rather than worry about collection of money, worry about talking to your attorney about litigation. This might be a major risk for liability. Have complaining patients elaborate as to why they feel this way. Try to solve the problem, but only within the limitations of your authority. You could recommend they set up a meeting with the doctor or even get the doctor right then. Often, when you see major malpractice cases, they develop from this type of dialog. If your documentation is poor, and it often is, you can encounter problems down the road. When patients feel they didn't get proper care or treatment, in almost every case the judge and jury will rule in their favor.

***The insurance company said you charged too much. They did not pay your whole bill.***

Ask if they were satisfied with the care they had been provided. Explain the basis used for determining your fees and how they fit into the prevailing fees for your geographic and practice area. Show them a separate brochure that explains how fees are developed and how Medicare works in a very basic sense. You could suggest they go and check around. They come back to you because they understand you deliver quality care, you are reasonable and you are their doctor.

***My husband is supposed to pay this or my parents are supposed to pay this.***

If a child is involved, the parent who brings the patient is responsible for the bill. If an adult is involved, the patient is to pay the bill. In both cases, they are responsible for collecting from the absent, responsible party. Your contract for treatment is not with the absent, responsible party. The physician is not a party to the disillusionment action. All of this should be covered during the intake interview. Divorce situations and university settings both involve absent responsible parties. University towns are so difficult because you are dealing with students who are covered by their parents' insurance.

***I know nothing about this. I never received any of your statements.***

Of course, your statements should include address correction requested, changes made, acknowledgments, point of certification, and new address, if applicable. Rather than argue over whether they received your statements, just verify the demographic information, restate the balance due, and the date of service, and request that a check be issued today. Send a statement with a handwritten note explaining that a phone call will be made within two days to verify the check was mailed.

Nothing is wrong with using the telephone. But, when are people home to talk to you? They are home the same time you are home. You need to create a policy by which someone calls your patients during evening hours. If you call after 9:00 p.m., you will be breaking federal law. However, if you call between 5:00 p.m. and 9:00 p.m., you can usually catch people at home. The best two nights, without exception, are Monday and Thursday. Studies have shown these are the two best days Monday falls after the weekend and Thursday is before the weekend. No one is usually home on Friday nights and for that matter as a general rule, making weekend calls is normally a waste of your time.

## Telephone Collection Tips

- Ensure you are talking with the person responsible for payment of the bill. Never discuss the account with anybody except the responsible party. Make sure you abide by this federal law.
- Identify yourself.
- State your reason for calling.
- Listen.
- Explore the possibilities of a loan or other source of financial support.
- Obtain a firm commitment as to when the payment will be received (a specific day or date).

## Objectives

- Arranging payment that is agreeable to you and the patient.
- Gathering asset information to support the physician if legal action is taken. This is vital information if skip tracing becomes necessary.
- Credit references.
- In-law information.
- Collection of the balance due and retaining that money in the practice.
- Listening well and identifying the debtor type.
- Utilizing pressure points if appropriate.
- Controlling the conversation.
- Using long, silent pauses to encourage the debtor to talk. Silence is an excellent tool.
- Never becoming hostile. If a debtor becomes agitated, slow your speech… lower your voice…force the listener to calm down and pay attention.
- Updating credit information.

- Verifying debtor demographics and employment.
- Making copious notes. If they say they are going to pay you next Tuesday, then make sure they pay you next Tuesday. Mark your calendar. Follow up on these promises.
- Offering alternatives for payment.
- Being flexible. A small weekly or monthly payment is better than no payment at all.
- Following up to be sure commitments are kept.
- Being cautious to avoid an accusation of harassment.
- Making note of what time you call. It is very clearly noted in the law that if you call before 9:00 a.m. you are in violation of the law. Think about that. Ask your attorney to get you a copy of the public law and collections protocols.
- If you call after 9:00 p.m., you are in violation. Also, never call on Sunday and never call on a holiday.
- Frequency of calling will be noted. Calling on the job is absolutely prohibited.
- Empty threats will never work.
- Don't threaten if you don't follow through. If you are sending out statements at 120 days that say, "If you don't pay me, we are going to an agency for collections" and you don't ever send an account to a collection agency, you are in violation of the law. If a patient sues you, his or her attorney would raise this against you. The law states you must do what you said you will do. If your office policies are in place and you adhere to these policies, you have nothing to worry about.

## Motivating Phrases

- Have you sent your payment as promised? How did you send it? In order to keep your account on a current basis, we need to have your check in the office by Friday.
- I will be reviewing the accounts with the doctor on Friday and would like to show the doctor your good intentions to pay the debt.
- On Friday your account will be referred to a collection agency. (Again, it is best to have this in writing.)
- If you mail your check today, you can avoid the additional expense and embarrassment.
- The collection agency picks up all our delinquent accounts this Friday. I know you don't want yours included. Can you bring in your payment by Thursday? (The key to success is documentation and tracking. Does your staff member do that?)

Has your doctor spoken to patients relative to their bills? You don't necessarily want the doctor involved in the financial discussion, but if you have a tough account, the doctor is the perfect liaison with that patient. Patients will typically pay at the snap of a finger because they are humbled in the presence of the doctor. They are embarrassed by a confrontation with the doctor. Patients know the doctor has treated/cured their problem, but they haven't reimbursed him for his services. It's usually inappropriate to involve doctors, but on occasion it can be useful.

## "Never" Rules (Directly from Federal Law)

- Never threaten action you do not intend to take. Never use obscene, profane or abusive language.
- Never raise your voice or show anger.
- Never discuss the bill with anyone other than the responsible party.
- Never contact a debtor who has legal representation unless the attorney consents. Your attorney should contact the debtor's attorney.
- Never misrepresent yourself.
- Never charge interest or an additional fee unless agreed upon prior to treatment.
- Never communicate by unsealed envelopes or postcards.

## Recommendations:

- Every patient should receive a **monthly statement of account**. There are a number of billing options. You can do all the billing in-house or use commercial photocopy services. There are also commercial statement services that a lot of practices use. If you use a commercial statement service, continue to manage your accounts receivable issues from your office.
- If your system allows it, you should bill weekly. You can even do it daily by an alpha system. This simplifies the billing for your staff instead of trying to do all statements at the end of the month. Weekly billing also keeps the cash flow going. Have you ever noticed what happens in your office the day after statements hit? You usually get numerous phone calls from patients. By spreading out the billing, you can better manage those calls over a period of time.
- **Handwrite collection messages on statements**. A little personal touch goes a long, long way. It is much easier to ignore a computerized message or one that is stamped on the bottom. Handwritten collection notices mean the account is getting personal attention. The patient will know someone in your office reviewed the statement and wrote the message, which may give it a little more impact. Sample messages might be:
    - *"We missed your payment last month, please send one today."*

- *"Please let us know if you will need to arrange a payment schedule. We will be happy to do it."*
- ***"A payment sent today will prevent damage to your credit rating."*** Most people get very upset about this, because they do not want to have their credit rating damaged.

## Accounts Receivable Policy

The Truth-in-Lending Laws must be followed. From 1–30 days, you send statements only; for 31–60 days, add a handwritten note on the statement; and for 60–90 days, a telephone call needs to be made to the patient. Actually, by the 60th day, you should be on the phone. This is going to be harder to accomplish, because you may have to work overtime to reach people during the hours they are home. At 75 days, you need to arrange a payment agreement and have that signed. At 90 days, you need to send a letter stating collection action will occur 10 days later and send the letter return receipt certified. At 100 total days, the patient account should go to collection.

## Payment Plans

If a patient needs to go on a payment plan, you should have an established form for this purpose. First, you should send a letter to the patient once a payment is missed. After two missed payments, the account should go to collection. For non-sufficient checks, you should charge administrative expenses and check face value back to the account. You should demand cash payment on bad checks within ten days. You should then require that all future payments must be made in cash or with a money order.

A suggested payment agreement document for accounts requiring less than 4 payments (if you receive more than 4 payments, the Truth-in-Lending Laws take effect) that will usually hold up in court might be:

> *I __________(patient) agree to pay the sum of $50 per week or month on my account balance of $_________. This will be payable on the __________ (day of the week/month) beginning __________. I agree that failure to comply with this agreement will result in collection action. I am responsible for the payment and I sign and I date this agreement.*

When you have an account requiring more than four payments, you get into Truth-in-Lending Laws as well as disclosures and compliance laws. The patient's name must be listed, responsible party, address, and phone (daytime and evening), and then you need to list cash price, medical fee, less cash discount, unpaid balance of cash price, amount financed because you are becoming a financial institution, finance charge, total of payments, deferred payment, and the annual percentage rate. You state that the total payments listed are payable to Dr. Doe at the above address, in so many monthly payments, beginning date, the amount for each payment, when all consecutive payments are due, etc. Wording should be included relative to "failure to comply with this agreement will result in collection action and responsibility for the court costs." This will usually hold up every time.

## Release of Patient

There has been a recent change in philosophy regarding patient release for non-payment because of increased litigation against physicians and hospitals regarding patient dumping or abandonment. For this reason, we are advising all clients to consider these facts before releasing a patient from their care solely based on non-payment of the bill. However, if the patient is not being compliant with recommended treatment, there are sufficient grounds for release. Before releasing a patient for any reason, advise him or her to select another physician for continuing medical attention. Offer to provide a source for another physician. Inform such patients that you must have written authorization to have their records transferred. If they have a condition that requires constant medical attention, you must care for them until they are under the care of another doctor. You must keep them on your records for 30 days, as a general rule.

If the patient attempts to return to you for care after the account has been rendered to the agency or legal counsel, your staff may handle the situation with a reminder about the unpaid balance. Request cash payment prior to a scheduled appointment and/or advise the patient that cash payment is required for all future visits. Those are the ways that you can bring patients back into the practice. But remember, if you allow them to come back with a bad debt that is not resolved, you not only have an educational problem, you have a legal problem in terms of the public law of collectability.

The federal law states that if you send someone to a collection agency or an attorney, you cannot let them back in the practice until they pay their previous balance. Notation must be made on the patient chart concerning your actions. Be very careful when you send files or information to the collection agency; remember that the case might end up before a judge and a jury.

## Write-offs

Follow proper accounting procedures by charging the full amount and writing off the discounted amount. Deal with indigent care in your write-off category. Also deal with professional courtesy in your write-off category.

## Insurance Checks Sent to the Patient

It is a real problem when the insurance company sends payments to patients instead of you. Inform these patients that the insurance company will be making payment directly to them, but that you expect to be reimbursed for your services. If a patient receives an insurance check and keeps it or does not remit the balance in full, you should send a collection letter as well. A sample of the letter wording is as follows:

*We've been informed by your insurance carrier that payment for services rendered to you by Dr. Doe on _________(date) at this office has been sent directly to you. The total amount due for these services is $__________. We want to work with you for a convenient, comfortable settlement of the debt, but we cannot do this without your cooperation. Please send us the check by return mail. If we do not receive the check by __________(date), we will be forced to pursue collection action.*

## Children of Divorced Parents

Make sure your staff has clarified office policy prior to providing service to children of divorced parents. Obtain a written agreement or understanding of the policy and responsibility for payment. With insurance, verify coverage, insist on payment, accept assignment if applicable, and ensure the provider will receive payment directly.

## Workmen's Compensation Cases

Obtain verification of coverage from the employer with date of injury. Workmen's compensation can be a major headache. Obtain the name, address, telephone number and policy number of the insurance carrier for workmen's comp as well as health insurance coverage in case the claim is denied. Also, have the patient sign acknowledgment of responsibility in case the case is denied. Remember, the patient was injured while working. You cannot bill the patient for the debt unless the claim is ruled non-industrial. If the claim is referred to the workmen's compensation appeal board, you cannot bill the patient until there is a ruling on the case. Check with the patient for the case ruling and the day it was settled, and then you may bill the patient, with assignment of benefits on the account. Because settlement will sometimes go directly to patients, in worker's compensation cases, you should always assign benefits.

## Personal Injury Litigation

Obtain the name, address and telephone number of the attorney handling personal injury litigation. Have the patient sign a legal lien after explaining patient responsibility.

## Estate Debts

Estate debt involves multiple points. Proof of claim must be filed in the deceased person's probate. File the claim with the state administrator or legal representative. File a probate form with the appropriate court. If you do it quickly enough, you can be paid before the mortgage. They do not prioritize the bills, so get your bill in quickly and you will have a better chance of being paid. Watch the newspapers for notification of estate activity or settlement. If the executor rejects the debt, you can sue the estate in probate court. If there is a surviving spouse, the debt would have been jointly responsible by both prior to the death of the patient. The spouse is fully liable if you miss filing a claim in probate.

## Bankruptcy Filings

Upon receipt of a bankruptcy notice or adjustment of debt, federal law restrains you from billing the patient. Generally a patient filing straight bankruptcy has little or no assets and, as an unsecured creditor, you should probably just forget it and write the amount off. Write-off of an uncollectible debt is probably appropriate if the court fails to grant the debtor a discharge. Then, you may take any action necessary to collect the debt.

## Summary

As we have discussed, there is a three-pronged approach to accounts receivable, and collections are a separate issue. Accounts receivable management can deal with insurance companies, patients and bad debt, whether you use collection agencies or attorneys. How you approach your receivables is a state of mind, but it is also a state of the pocketbook. One of the most important things to remember is to have written policies that define the exact timeframes for each level of accounts receivable. Be sure you are aware of the current laws relative to collection letters and statements.

Review your policies with all staff members, and make sure all become involved in educating patients on payment and collection of fees. Make one person or department responsible for handling accounts receivable issues, questions and problems. Look at your individual practice and examine ways to improve collecting money due for the services rendered. Remember, the process begins with the first contact made with the patient and continues through every contact at the practice until the patient leaves and the bill is paid.

Remember too, the longer the accounts go without being paid, the more money the practice loses, until eventually you cannot recoup your costs. Be aggressive, but be aware of federal guidelines relative to collection procedures. The accounts receivable area of your practice is obviously one of the most important areas of the front office. It can greatly impact the success of your cash flow and ultimately your income bottom line, so make sure you give it the attention and importance it deserves.

Chapter 3

# Team Leadership & Standard Operating Procedures

*No one knows everything there is to know about the operation of your practice, but a Standard Operating Procedure manual will allow the staff to have a basic understanding of general operations.*

When the economy is in turmoil as it has been for a couple of years, ophthalmologists all want to know the secret to making their practice more efficient and profitable. The purpose of this chapter is to lay the groundwork for more effective practice management.

Our most economical and feasible marketing resources are "happy patients." What better way to promote your practice is there than word-of-mouth? You want your patients to walk out of the office and tell everyone they know what a wonderful experience they had. How do you accomplish this?

There are two good means to making the practice run smoothly and effectively. You need to establish Team Leaders and Standard Operating Procedures (SOPs). You have to have a well-trained staff with strong leaders who know what to do and when to do it.

## Team Leaders

Can your office operate without an office manager or practice administrator? Team leaders can be valuable to the successful day-to-day operation of your practice. These team leaders head up the various departments or areas of your practice. Each leader must be chosen carefully after objectives and goals are clearly outlined for each group or area. The office manager or the physicians should facilitate the selection of team leaders. A good team leader can have a positive and a powerful impact on a team, but on the other hand, a poor leader can ruin a project.

Gaining the support and confidence of the physicians and team members is critical for team leaders. It requires openness and understanding with their teams, and they should listen to suggestions and concerns, and be able to work with their teams to achieve goals. The team leader must be a skilled, two-way communicator, be able to listen, ask the right questions, and provide essential information to the physicians as well as the team.

The team leader is responsible for monitoring duties assigned to ensure employees are performing their jobs in a manner designed to maintain a high level of patient care and efficiency. Responsibility lies with team leaders to maintain an efficient flow of work by evaluating procedures accordingly. They also must be able to think clearly and exercise good judgment in initiating business and office policies. The leader should have the ability to standardize procedures and initiate changes when necessary.

Constantly reviewing procedures to strive for more efficient ways to conduct business, team leaders should also be striving for improved patient care. By doing this, they help establish, implement, revise, and carry out procedures, policies and operating procedures. They should also be responsible for creating and administering an on-the-job training program for new and current employees, as required. With flexibility a requirement, they must also be willing to perform other duties as directed by the management or the physicians. These are people who will make things happen and who will help keep everyone pulling in the same direction. The team leader is the bridge between management and the team.

The leader must engender trust among team members and, at the same time, with senior management. The leader strives to keep all team members enthused and involved at all times, while seeking to bring out their best performance. It is important to remember that a good leader has an unwavering belief in the success of the practice and an ability to lead a group of individuals without getting in their way.

## Good Team Leaders Strive to Have:

- An ability to delegate and keep people enthused
- A clear vision of the practice
- Political savvy
- A willingness to listen
- Problem solving skills
- An ability to resolve conflict
- Critical path project management skills
- Meeting management skills

- Dedication to the project, the team and the practice
- A willingness to empower people
- Respect for team members
- Plenty of energy
- Credibility with the team membership
- Good writing skills
- Oral presentation skills
- Good understanding of cash flow management
- An ability to roll with the punches

## Qualifications

Nowhere is it written that the team leader needs a college degree. What matters most is that the person has the right skills and an enthusiasm for the role. To be a successful team leader, the person must possess a clear mandate, with support from the senior management and physicians, to manage all policies and procedures. Throughout the month, each team leader should appear monthly before management or the physicians to provide a brief update concerning the team's activities.

When facing difficult problems, leaders should be able to get help easily; they should be free to go to management or the physicians whenever they feel it is necessary. The manager or physician who has a vested interest in the practice will usually do everything possible to help the team leader. In most cases, however, the best help for the team leader is from other team members. If there is good team spirit, other team members will be more than willing to help their leader.

Physicians and management must remember that being a team leader will intrinsically add 10-20% more time to the leader's work load, so they should keep that in mind if they are thinking of adding more work to the team leader's schedule.

## Standard Operating Procedures

A Standard Operating Procedure (SOP) is a detailed written set of procedures for all employees to follow which outlines the correct way to handle almost every situation that could arise, in any division of the office. A Standard Operating Procedure Manual is typically made for each employee to review, providing them a clear understanding of the correct procedure to take when a problem arises.

SOPs can be as general as how to appropriately greet a patient, customer or sales person, or as specific as how and when to contact a physician who is out of the office. The SOP Manual would list beeper numbers, cell phone numbers or home phone numbers explaining how to handle the situation if there is no response within a certain amount of time. Whereas a job description is a broad description of the job you've been hired to perform, a Standard Operating Procedure is a more detailed description of how to perform each function of the job and solve problems that may develop in a manner consistent with the practice's philosophy.

Standard Operating Procedures can also assist in training new employees, cross training other employees and employee evaluations. Staff should always have administrative guidance, but these are a good foundation for explaining basic procedures and as a reference for handling specific situations. Someone should always be available if a major problem develops, but minor issues shouldn't monopolize the administrator's time if the staff can correctly solve the problem. Employees can more easily handle the day-to-day procedures and solve minor problems with this reference tool available.

Standard Operating Procedures, which need to be clear, concise and detailed, should be implemented and shared with new employees at the date of hire. Offices tend to run more efficiently with these procedures in place. SOPs can be modified from time to time if an employee discovers a more efficient way the job can be performed.

All employees should be expected to know and understand SOPs. They not only make the office run more efficiently, but if you have more than one location, it will ensure conformity at all of your locations. This will be a cost effective manual because your staff will be able to rotate locations and know what is expected at each of the practice locations.

Programs such as this will free up some of the administrator's time to focus on his or her own tasks and responsibilities. Not all of your employees will use every SOP, but the manual should be accessible to all employees so that they are familiar with the operation of the practice. No one knows everything there is to know about the operation of your practice, but an SOP Manual will allow the staff to have a basic understanding of general operations.

How do you begin compiling your manual? First, you have to know what every single person does in the practice every day. The manual will be a work in progress for several months while you fine-tune it. You will need feedback from all of your staff, but especially from your team leaders and physicians. If your team leaders complete their protocols first, they can set a precedent for the entire staff.

The SOP Manual should include instructions and guidelines relative to all areas of the office:

## Communications

- Handling incoming calls for physicians (typical replies)
- Handling incoming calls for physicians (decision tree)
- Internal calls
- Taking phone messages

- Telephone etiquette
- Protocol for weekend calls
- Protocol when no physician is available

## General Office Procedures

- Opening the office for business
- Checking patients in
- Checking patients out
- Closing the office for the day
- Collecting payments
- Dealing with cancellations
- Dealing with no shows
- Dictation by the doctors
- Front desk staffing
- Greeting the public
- Training plans
- Medical training for staff
- Ordering reprints, forms and letterhead
- Security
- Safety guidelines and practices
- Scheduling appointments
- Scheduling spreadsheets
- Scheduling hospital consults
- Scheduling surgeries

## Clinical Procedures

- Clinic routines

- Performing visual acuity
- Screening checklist
- Child screening
- Parameters for technicians

## Optical

- Contact lenses
- Contact lens pricing
- Delivery of optical
- Protocol for optical
- Sales of optical accessories
- Optical payments and collections

In the following pages, you will find a few sample SOP manual pages relative to some of the areas mentioned above. These may provide you with guidelines to create SOPs specific to your particular practice. These can be created and assembled for each area of the practice. Hopefully, these sample pages will help to serve as a template for your manual. Remember, these should be tailored to your specific practice and philosophy.

## Standard Operating Procedure Manual Sample Pages

### Taking Telephone Messages

**Policy**

The telephone is a critical communication tool at the practice. All telephone messages taken will be legibly written on a form designed specifically for taking telephone messages and will include: the name of the caller, the name of the patient, the date and time of the call, and the message itself.

**Procedure**

1. Staff will answer the phone in a warm professional manner as outlined in the procedure for answering the telephone.
2. All messages are to be written legibly on a designated telephone message document.
3. If an established patient telephones, the front office staff will pull the medical

record for the Clinic Team Leader or designee and take the chart to that area or Department.

4. If there is an urgent call, the appropriate Team Leader should be notified for disposition of the call.

5. All doctors personally asking to speak with any physician regarding an established or potential new patient, who needs to be seen that day, should be directed to the physician who will be taking the add-on by using the paging system.

6. If a physician calls for a specific physician who is in surgery for the day, the calling physician will be notified of that fact. If another physician is in the office, the staff is to offer to connect the calling physician to that physician.

7. If the calling physician wishes to only speak with a specific physician, the staff will leave a written message for the physician in the dictation station. The message will contain: the name of the doctor calling, the date and time of the call, the name of the patient, and if the patient is established to the practice. If the call is regarding a consultation or urgent issue, call the doctor's location, if known.

## Greeting the Public

**Policy**

All members of the public, including patients, families, vendors, drug company representatives and delivery persons, are to be acknowledged by the check-in staff in a warm, friendly and professional manner.

**Procedure**

1. The staff will greet persons presenting to the front desk with either: "Good morning, how may I help you?" or "Good afternoon, how may I help you?"

2. Staff at the front desk will address all adult patients and their families using the appropriate titles, Mr., Mrs., Ms., Miss, Dr., Father, etc., in addition to the patient's last name unless instructed to do otherwise by the patient or family member.

3. Staff will ask the person what he or she in the office for, and if it is for an appointment, ask for the appointment time.

4. If a patient is more than twenty minutes late for his or her appointment, the clinic staff will be notified. If the patient then comes into the office, tenured clinic staff will be notified and will determine whether or not the patient can be seen on that day. If the patient cannot be seen due to tardiness, the patient will be rescheduled and/or placed on the cancellation list.

5. Staff at the front desk will be in close contact with the clinic staff and will notify waiting patients and families if the physician they are scheduled to see is more than thirty minutes behind schedule, in order to offer an opportunity for the patient to reschedule to a later date.

6. Technicians should notify the front desk of how the physicians are doing throughout the day.

## Dealing With No-Show Patients

**Policy**

An appointment with the doctor is important to the eye health and well being of the patient. It is the policy of this practice to prevent as many no-show appointments as possible by confirming all patient appointments no more than 24 hours in advance.

**Procedure**

1. If the patient does not appear for a scheduled appointment, a call will be placed within 24 hours in order to reschedule the appointment.
2. The patient's name is to be entered onto the "no-show log" for the appropriate physician. The no-show log is maintained during the week and presented to the physician every Friday.
3. A notation is to be placed in the medical record under "phone messages" that the patient was called and the appointment rescheduled. If the patient prefers to not reschedule the appointment, try to ascertain why.
4. If the patient was not reached to reschedule, leave a voice mail message or answering machine message, if possible.
5. Staff will always attempt to speak directly with the patient or a responsible party.
6. If you could not reach the patient by phone, you should send a post card letting the patient know he or she missed a scheduled appointment and should call the office to reschedule.

## Contact Lens Protocol

**Policy**

It is the policy of this practice to professionally and competently serve all patient customers who seek to order, reorder refit, be trained on insertion and removal of contact lenses, or be checked for contact lenses, as directed by the physician.

**Procedure**

1. Staff will greet the patient and introduce themselves in a warm, professional manner using the patient's name and the appropriate title. The staff will ask the patient how he or she can be helped. If the patient is there for a contact lens fitting, staff must have the patient sign a form acknowledging there will be a charge for the lens fitting.
2. The staff will ask the patient if he or she has worn contact lenses in the past.
3. The staff will seat the patient and/or responsible party while the Contact Lens

Optician pulls the patient's medical record.

4. The staff will review the patient chart for physician instructions as to lens type and prescription. If there are no specifications, the staff will explain all the different types of lenses and the pricing, as well as the payment policy.

5. The staff will discuss advantages and disadvantages of all lenses with the patient and/or responsible party.

6. The staff will ask the patient and/or responsible party if they have a lens preference. The staff will then fit accordingly. If there is no preference, the staff will fit the lenses that will most likely fit the patient's lifestyle, taking into consideration the patient's prescription, age and maturity level, extracurricular activities and sports involvement.

7. The staff will encourage the patient to remain in the lenses fitted for at least two weeks, but if the patient feels he or she cannot do this, the patient will need to call the office to set up another appointment.

8. Once a contact lens fit has been completed and if the lenses are in stock, the patient is instructed on Insertion and Removal (I & R) of the lenses. The patient is also trained on the cleaning and care of the lenses. The staff will give the patient a starter kit, which includes a case and solution.

9. If the lenses are not available in the office, the staff will tell the patient that it will take five to seven days for delivery of the lenses.

10. The staff will ask the patient to schedule an appointment to see the Contact Lens Optician again in approximately one week for insertion and pick-up. The patient may alternately be encouraged to call one hour in advance if unable to keep the follow-up appointment.

11. If the patient is being seen for a contact lens check only, the staff will communicate what they are doing, why it is being done and what is found, if anything. The staff will also instruct the patient and/or responsible party if anything else needs to be done.

12. If a patient or responsible part only needs lenses re-ordered, the staff will check to see if the lenses needed are in stock. If the lenses are not in stock, the patient or responsible party will be told that it will take five to seven days for the lenses to be received. The lenses can either be mailed directly to the patient for a $5.00 fee or picked up at the office. The lenses can also be sent overnight, if needed, which will cost an additional $15.00. The office should collect the extra charge to mail contact lenses at this time.

13. The staff will always encourage the sale of back-up glasses and/or sunglasses for all patients purchasing contact lenses. The staff will mention current sales promotions to promote further sales in the optical department.

## Delivery of Opticals

**Policy**

It is the policy of the office to expedite the delivery of all optical orders and to ensure that the prescription is correctly made.

**Procedure**

1. When an order is delivered from the optical lab, the prescription is checked against the order.
2. The optical staff will contact the patient and notify him or her that the order has been delivered.
3. The staff will tell the patient what the account balance is when calling, and remind the patient the office accepts checks, debit cards and credit cards.
4. No optical order is to be released until the account balance is satisfied in full.
5. Generally no payment arrangements are permitted on optical orders. Unusual circumstances will be dealt with on a case-by-case basis by the optical department Team Leader in conjunction with the physician.

Chapter 4

# Coding and Pricing

*Correct coding has a significant impact on the physician's reimbursement, and it reduces the potential for fraud and abuse exposure.*

Why is it important to code correctly? Because, the physician's practice then receives the maximum legal reimbursement for physician services. This chapter will examine the different types of coding as well as discuss documentation that justifies the coding level. CPT and HCPCS codes are used to properly code for medical procedures, supplies and materials physicians use. Correct coding has a significant impact on the physician's reimbursement, and it reduces the potential for fraud and abuse exposure.

## CPT CODING

The first volume of CPT codes was published in 1966 by the American Medical Association. Current Procedural Terminology (CPT) was developed to provide a standard and uniform language to communicate among physicians and third-party payers. This coding system is a listing of over 10,000 codes, descriptions used for reporting medical services, and procedures performed by physicians and other health care professionals. CPT coding is also used for claims processing and for the development of medical review guidelines. The American Medical Association annually publishes CPT codes to reflect new procedure codes, delete obsolete codes or change current descriptions to reflect procedural changes. Medicare and Medicaid programs mandate the use of CPT codes, which all commercial carriers follow.

### Fundamentals of CPT coding:

CPT codes are five-digit numeric codes [i.e. CPT 27130 Arthroplasty, Acetabular and Proximal Femoral Prosthetic Replacement (Total Hip Replacement), with or without autograft or allograft)], thereby simplifying the reimbursement process for insurance carriers and eliminating the need for lengthy reports.

CPT codes, which describe procedures and services, are required by all insurance and commercial carriers. CPT codes are reviewed and revised annually and are divided into six sections. They are:

| | |
|---|---|
| **Evaluation and Management** | **99200 – 99499** |
| **Anesthesiology** | **00100 – 01999** |
| **Surgery** | **10040 – 66979** |
| **Radiology** | **70010 – 79999** |
| **Pathology and Laboratory** | **80002 – 89399** |
| **Medicine** | **90701 – 99199** |

Each section is then subdivided into anatomical, diagnostic and procedural subheadings. There are hundreds of changes every year, and there are now more than 7500 codes. Read your medical bulletins and note applicable comments by the codes in your CPT book.

## ICD-9 CODING

ICD-9 stands for International Classification of Diseases, the Ninth Revision, a statistic classification system. This system groups diseases and conditions into restrictive categories to allow statistical analysis and retrieval. There must be only one place in which the disease or condition can be classified. This statistical classification system began as an effort to determine the causes of deaths in England in the $17^{th}$ century. Between the $17^{th}$ and $18^{th}$ centuries, many other efforts were made to classify causes of diseases and illnesses. In 1837, a system was devised to classify diseases by anatomical site. This classification principal is used today and forms the basis of the international list of causes of death.

In the late 1970s, the National Center of Health Statistics compiled the ICD – Ninth Edition. This included more specificity of diseases/conditions than previously available and the addition of codes to include ambulatory care and hospital settings.

Unlike the CPT codes, ICD-9 is not used for reimbursement. However, it is used in conjunction with CPT codes to justify the CPT code use. CPT codes do not reflect diseases or conditions, but rather the services and procedures performed for those conditions. Since April 1, 1989, physicians have been required to submit ICD-9 codes on all claims for Medicare services provided under the Part B series. Other carriers also request the diagnosis submitted with the ICD-9 codes. Alphabetical indexes assist physicians and their staff in locating correct codes for presenting problems, conditions, known diseases of the patient, reasons for health care encounters, and two supplementary classifications: V-codes, for factors influencing health status, and E-codes, for external causes of injury and poisoning. ICD-9 codes have evolved into a five-digit numeric coding system. Medicare and other carriers require that ICD-9 codes be reported to the highest level of specificity.

## Fundamentals of ICD-9 Coding

ICD-9 coding is mandatory for Medicare, Medicaid and commercial carrier billing. ICD codes identify: patient presenting problem, symptoms, disease state, condition, and history (personal and/or family).

ICD-9 requires codes be used to their highest 5-digit specificity where available. For example:

825 – Fracture of one or more tarsal and metatarsal bones

825.3 – Fracture of other tarsal and metatarsal bones, open

825.33 – Cuboid

Additional classifications included in the ICD-9 system are: morphology of neoplasms, glossary of mental disorders, and classification of drugs and industrial accidents according to agency. These appendices are included as a reference to provide further information about the patient's circumstances to determine a diagnostic statement, maintain a tumor registry, and aid in classifying new drugs.

Proper coding is important for physicians to ensure the highest legal reimbursement while reducing exposure to fraud and abuse. Physicians and their staff members are responsible for properly coding the services that they provide. This is a primary concern of Medicare and the HCFA because of the misuse and fraudulent reimbursement that has been found in the medical community. For these reasons, it is paramount that physicians and their staff are trained annually in the current CPT and ICD-9 codes. The ICD-9 is updated annually in October. Medicare allows a 90-day grace period.

## HCPCS CODING

HCPCS is an acronym for **H**CFA **C**ommon **P**rocedure **C**oding **S**ystem. This was developed in 1983 by the Health Care Finance Administration (HCFA) to standardize coding used for processing Medicare claims. These Level II alphanumeric codes are for services not covered by CPT. These include physician services and non-physician services such as ambulance, audiology, physical therapy, speech pathology, vision care, drugs, and supplies, DME equipment, prosthetics, and orthotics.

These are five-unit codes with the first unit a letter of the alphabet: A, B, C, D, E, H, J, L, M, P, Q, R and V. There were 1,554 HCPCS codes as of July 1998. HCPCS codes beginning with the letter Q are reserved for use by HCFA.

## Evaluation and Management Codes

Here we will cover some of the principles involved in coding for physicians' offices in regard to billing practices. In 1992, a new segment was added regarding Evaluation and Management (E/M) coding. This segment is primarily important to the physician for securing appropriate reimbursement for the services he provides.

The basic format of the E/M services involves patient history, examination and decision-making tools. In order to arrive at the appropriate code to apply to E/M services, the physician must first evaluate whether the patient is new or established as well as the level of service being performed. Detailed information is necessary to assess the appropriate level of service (as defined by the six category descriptors):

1. The level of the history of the patient
2. The level of examination
3. The decision-making components, whether or not counseling is provided
4. Whether coordination of care is included in the service
5. The nature of the presenting problem
6. The amount of time to provide the service

## Definition of Terms

### History

| | |
|---|---|
| **Problem Focused (PF)** | ☐ chief complaint; brief history of present illness or problem. |
| **Expanded Problem Focused (EPF)** | ☐ PF plus problem-pertinent system review. |
| **Detailed (D)** | ☐ chief complaint; extended history of present illness; problem pertinent system review extended to include a review of a limited number of additional systems; **pertinent** past, family and/or social history *directly related to the patient's problems.* |
| **Comprehensive (C)** | ☐ chief complaint; extended history of present illness; review of systems that is directly related to the problem(s) identified in the history of the present illness plus a review of all additional body systems; **complete** past, family and social history. |

## Type of Exam

| | |
|---|---|
| **Problem Focused (PF)** | ☐ an examination that is limited to the affected body area or organ system. |
| **Expanded Problem Focused (EPF)** | ☐ PF plus other symptomatic or related organ systems. |
| **Detailed (D)** | ☐ an extended examination of the affected body area(s) and other symptomatic or related system(s). |
| **Comprehensive (C)** | ☐ a general multi-system examination or a complete examination of a single organ system. **Note:** The comprehensive examination performed as part of the preventative medicine evaluation and management service is multi-system, but its extent is based on age and risk factors identified. |

## Type of Decision-making

For a service to qualify as involving a certain type of medical decision-making, two of the three descriptions listed after each type of decision-making must be met or exceeded.

| | Number of Diagnoses or Management Options | Amount and/or Complexity of Data to be Reviewed | Risk of Complications or Mortality and/or Morbidity |
|---|---|---|---|
| **Straight Forward (SF)** | Minimal | Minimal or None | Minimal |
| **Low Complexity (LC)** | Limited | Limited | Low |
| **Moderate Complexity (MC)** | Multiple | Moderate | Moderate |
| **High Complexity (HC)** | Extensive | Extensive | High |

| CPT recognized body areas: | CPT recognized organ systems | |
|---|---|---|
| * Head, including the face | * Eyes | * Neurologic |
| * Neck | * Ears, Nose, Mouth and Throat | * Skin |
| * Chest, including breasts and axilla | * Cardiovascular | * Psychiatric |
| * Abdomen<br>• Genitalia, groin, buttocks | * Respiratory<br>* Gastrointestinal | * Hematologic/ Lymphatic<br>* Immunologic |
| * Back<br>* Each extremity | * Genitourinary<br>* Musculoskeletal | |

# Outpatient Evaluation and Management Codes

## Select the Appropriate E/M Code

Based upon information recorded above, check the appropriate level of care box below and document it in the patient's record. For the following code series listed below—office/OH new patients, OB status, initial hospital, office/OH consultations, IH consultations, emergency department services—all 3 KEY components must be met or exceeded to qualify for a given level of care (only 2 of 3 for the remaining code series).

## Office/OH New Patient

| | 99201 | 99202 | 99203 | 99204 | 99205 |
|---|---|---|---|---|---|
| History | PF | EPF | D | C | C |
| Examination | PF | EPF | D | C | C |
| Decision-making | SF | SF | LC | MC | HC |

## Office/OH Established Patient

| | 99211 | 99212 | 99213 | 99214 | 99215 |
|---|---|---|---|---|---|
| History | □ | PF | EPF | D | C |
| Examination | □ | PF | EPF | D | C |
| Decision-making | □ | SF | LC | MC | HC |

## Office/OH Consultation

| | 99241 | 99242 | 99243 | 99244 | 99245 |
|---|---|---|---|---|---|
| History | PF | EPF | D | C | C |
| Examination | PF | EPF | D | C | C |
| Decision-making | SF | SF | LC | MC | HC |

## Care Plan Oversight Services

Within a 30-day period, revision of care plans of patients requiring complex or multidisciplinary care of home health agencies or hospice.

| | |
|---|---|
| 99375 | 30–60 minutes |
| 99376 | greater than 60 minutes |

| Basic Life and/or Disability Evaluation Services | Work Related Medical Disability Evaluation Services | |
|---|---|---|
| **99450** includes: | **99455** by the treating physician that includes: | **99456** by other then the treating physician that includes: |
| * measurement of height, weight and blood pressure;<br>* completion of a medical history following a life insurance pro forma;<br>* collection of blood sample and/or urinalysis complying with "chain of custody" protocols; and<br>* completion of necessary documentation/certificates. | * completion of a medical history commensurate with the patient's condition;<br>* performance of an examination commensurate with the patient's condition;<br>* formulation of a diagnosis, assessment of capabilities and stability, and calculation of impairment;<br>* development of future medical treatment plan; and<br>* completion of necessary documentation/ certificates and report. | * completion of a medical history commensurate with the patient's condition;<br>* performance of an examination with the patient's condition;<br>* formulation of a diagnosis, assessment of capabilities and stability, and calculation of impairment;<br>* development of future medical treatment plan; and completion of necessary documentation /certi-ficates and report |

# Hospital Evaluation and Management Codes

## New or Established Patient Observation Services

| | 99218 | 99219 | 99220 |
|---|---|---|---|
| History | D/C | C | C |
| Examination | D/C | C | C |
| Decision-making | SF/L | MC | HC |

## Emergency Department Services

| | 99281 | 99282 | 99283 | 99284 | 99285 |
|---|---|---|---|---|---|
| History | PF | EPF | EPF | D | C |
| Examination | PF | EPF | EPF | D | C |
| Decision-making | SF | LC | MC | MC | HC |

**Observation care discharge day manage-date of discharge other than the initial 99217**

# Inpatient Evaluation and Management Codes

## Initial Hospital Care

| | 99221 | 99222 | 99223 |
|---|---|---|---|
| History | D/C | C | C |
| Examination | D/C | C | C |
| Decision-making | SF/L | MC | HC |

## Subsequent Hospital Care

| | 99231 | 99232 | 99233 |
|---|---|---|---|
| History | PF | EPF | D |
| Examination | PF | EPF | D |
| Decision-making | SF/L | MC | HC |

**Hospital discharge day management 99238**

## Initial Inpatient Consultation

| | 99251 | 99252 | 99253 | 99254 | 99255 |
|---|---|---|---|---|---|
| History | PF | EPF | D | C | C |
| Examination | PF | EPF | D | C | C |
| Decision-making | SF | SF | LC | MC | HC |

## Follow-up Inpatient Consultation

| | 99261 | 99262 | 99263 |
|---|---|---|---|
| History | PF | EPF | D |
| Examination | PF | EPF | D |
| Decision-making | SF/L | M | H |

## Distinguish Between a Consult and a Visit

In general, when billing for a consult versus an office visit, keep in mind who controls the patient's overall management. A consulting physician may evaluate the patient, order or perform diagnostic services, and start therapeutic service by writing orders. He or she would inform the other physician of the findings and recommendations, and because it is a consult, the patient would be returned to the first physician for any additional treatment and follow-up. If the patient's care is meant to be taken over by the doctor who did the evaluation or ordered diagnostic tests, etc., then the physician's service becomes an office visit, even if it is the patient's first visit.

Necessary components for a consult include:

* A request from a physician
* For a stated condition
* For advice or opinion

You will need the UPIN number of the referring physician on your claim forms. Both physicians need to have notes in the patient record regarding the referral. Most practices give their advice or opinion by way of a letter to the referring physician. Copies are retained in the patient chart. In general, this letter is not sufficient documentation for the <u>level</u> of care. Therefore, as required for all Evaluation and Management (E/M) codes, it is necessary to document the history, examination and decision-making.

## Office/OH Consultation

| Component | 99241 | 99242 | 99243 | 99244 | 99245 |
|---|---|---|---|---|---|
| History | PF | EPF | D | C | C |
| Examination | PF | EPF | D | C | C |
| Decision-making | SF | SF | LC | MC | HC |

## Second and Third Opinion

When a Medicare beneficiary is facing a "major procedure" such as cardiac catheterization or gastroscopy, the patient may request a second opinion and have it paid by Medicare.

When the first and second opinions differ, the patient may seek a third opinion and have this covered by Medicare.

When filing a second or third opinion, do not use the UPIN of the first doctor because the patient requested the service and Medicare does not recognize this as a referral situation.

Use codes 99271–99275 Confirmatory Consultations for new or established patients for any setting.

## Observation Codes

Physicians who admit to the observation beds in a hospital may bill with codes 99218, 99219 and 99220. The reimbursement is similar to initial hospital care codes.

Guidelines:

- Usually within 24 hours
- Must be an observation record with admit time, orders, nursing notes and physician progress notes (separate from ER record)
- Usually to determine if condition warrants an admission
- The admitting physician uses these codes; other physicians who see the patient must use outpatient consultation codes. (Internist admits, ask surgeon's opinion) (Surgeon admits, asks cardiologist's opinion).
- No inpatient consultation codes can be billed since the patient is not an inpatient
- Only one observation code is permitted per date of service. If discharge date is the same as the admit date, you may bill only one code.
- When observation services cover two dates, bill the appropriate code 99218–99220 and the discharge code 99217.
- When observation covers more than two dates, then outpatient visit codes must be used.

* When a patient is admitted for observation, only one code (initial hospital) is allowed for that date. The initial hospital code covers all care on that date from all sites.

* When observation occurs during a global period, they are not billable unless circumstances permit the use of modifier -24, -25 or -57.

## Emergency Department Services

When the ER physician asks a specialist to see a patient in the ER, the specialist bills a consultation code and gives advice to the referring physician. Later services are billed as visits, not follow-up consultations.

When the ER physician asks a specialist to see a patient in the specialist's office, the specialist should bill an office visit, because the patient was sent for care, not advice.

When the specialist (acting as primary care) sends the patient to the ER, and the ER physician asks the specialist to come to the ER to determine whether to admit the patient then:

— If admitted, the specialist bills the appropriate initial hospital care code (99221-99223) since all E&M services on that date are considered part of admission.

— If the patient is sent home, then the specialist and the ER physician both bill emergency department codes (99281–99285). As the primary physician, the specialist is responsible for the management of the patient and cannot bill consultation codes.

## Prolonged Services

| | | |
|---|---|---|
| **99354** | Outpatient Prolonged | 1st hour |
| **99355** | Outpatient Prolonged | Each additional ½ hour |
| **99356** | Inpatient Prolonged | 1st hour |
| **99357** | Inpatient Prolonged | Each additional ½ hour |

| PROLONGED SERVICES | |
|---|---|
| **Total Duration of Prolonged Services Face to Face** | **Code(s)** |
| **Less than 30 minutes**<br>*(less than ½ hour)* | Not reported separately |
| **30-74 minutes**<br>*(½ hr. - 1 hr. 14 min.)* | **99354 X 1** (First Hour) |
| **75-104 minutes**<br>*(1 hr. 15 min. - 1 hr. 44 min.)* | **99354 X 1** and **99355 X 1**<br>(Each additional ½ hour) |
| **105-134 minutes**<br>*(1 hr. 45 min. - 2 hr. 14 min.)* | **99354 X 1** and **99355 X 2** |
| **135-164 minutes**<br>*(2 hr. 15 min. - 2 hr. 44 min.)* | **99354 X 1** and **99355 X 3** |
| **165-194 minutes**<br>*(2 hr. 45 min. - 3 hr. 14 min.)* | **99354 X 1** and **99355 X 4** |

Medicare will pay the prolonged service codes (99355–99357) only when billed with the following E/M codes:

| | |
|---|---|
| **New Patient** | **99201–99205** |
| **Established Patient** | **99211–99215** |
| **Outpatient Consultation** | **99241–99245** |

Your documentation must clearly show the history, examination and decision-making to support the visit code, the duration and content of the prolonged service that is in addition to the usual time spent for the visit code. Medicare requires these services to be for direct face-to-face contact with the patient.

## Modifiers

Modifiers are used along with CPT codes. These two digit modifiers assist in further defining procedures/services rendered by physicians. They designate multiple procedures, reduced or unusual procedures performed, etc. The following is a listing of the 1994 modifiers physicians use:

**-20** Microsurgery: Indicates the use of an operating microscope. Include documentation showing necessity for microsurgery. No effect on payment.

**-21** Prolonged E/M services: Used with the highest level of E/M service, and indicates that more time and a greater level of intensity were required. No effect on payment.

**-22** Unusual services: required when surgical service is unusual and higher payment is requested. Documentation is necessary. (Note: You have two options when billing modifier –22. You can either include a reimbursement estimate of the amount you want Medicare to pay, or you can leave it to your carrier to decide. HCFA takes no stand on which is correct, but consultants often advise billers to put in an estimate, otherwise you are gambling your reimbursement dollars on your carrier's decision.)

**-23** Unusual anesthesia: A procedure normally calling for no anesthesia or local anesthesia, but requires general anesthesia.

**-24** Unrelated E/M service by the same physician during a post-op period: Visits unrelated to surgical procedure provided for unrelated diagnosis or condition.

**-25** Significant, separately identifiable E/M service by the same physician on the day of a minor surgical procedure.

**-26** Professional/physician component of a service: Indicates interpretation of diagnostic tests.

**-32** Mandated services: Related to mandated consultation.

**-47** Anesthesia by surgeon: Medicare does not cover this service.

**-50** Bilateral procedure: Used when unilateral procedures or diagnostic tests are done bilaterally. Payment will be 150% for surgical procedures and 200% for diagnostic tests.

**-51** Multiple surgeries by same physician on same day: The highest level procedure is paid at 100%, the second through fifth procedures will be paid at 50%. Any procedure beyond the fifth procedure would continue to be carrier-priced "by report" based on documentation. Don't use this modifier with evaluation and management services, and don't append it to designated add-on codes.

**-52** Reduced services: Indicates the service was less involved or eliminated. Documentation required. Payment may be reduced. Don't use this modifier for terminated services unless it's used to denote unusual or reduced services that terminated before anesthesia was started.

**-53** Discontinued procedure: Use this modifier when the physician decides to terminate a surgical or diagnostic procedure because of extenuating circumstances or those that threaten the well being of the patient. Report it with the code for the discontinued or diagnostic procedure. Reminder: Do not cut your own reimbursement. Just provide extensive documentation along with your claim that will help the carrier determine the amount you will be reimbursed.

**-54** Surgical care only: Indicates surgeon performed pre-op care and the surgical procedure, and a second physician provided post-op care. The surgeon is paid for pre- and intra-op percentages only.

**-55** Postoperative management only: Physician provides only post-op care and is paid based on post-op percentage only.

**-56** Preoperative management only: Physician provides only the pre-op care.

**-57** Visit or consult day before or day of major surgery, when decision for surgery was made during the visit.

**-58** Staged or related procedure or service by same physician during post-operative period.

**-59** Distinct procedural service: Indicates that a procedure or service was distinct or independent from other services performed on the same day. Report it with two procedures that are not usually reported together to show that they are both necessary under the circumstances. Use in place of the –GB modifier under the National Correct Coding Policy.

**-62** Two surgeons: Both surgeons should use modifier. Each physician receives 62.5% of payment. Documentation required.

**-66** Surgical team: Documentation required. Carrier determines payment.

**-76** Repeat procedure by the same physician.

**-77** Repeat procedure by another physician.

**-78** Return to the operating room for a related or unrelated procedure during the postoperative period: Used for complications of original surgery. Payment is reduced by 50%.

**-79** Unrelated procedure or service by the same physician during the postoperative period: Used for unrelated diagnosis or condition. No effect on payment.

**-80** Assistant surgeon: Payment based on 16% of fee schedule amount.

**-81** Minimum assistant surgeon: Not covered by Medicare.

**-82** Assistant surgeon: (When qualified resident surgeon is not available) Payment based on 16% of fee schedule.

**-90** Reference (Outside) laboratory.

**-99** Multiple modifiers.

**-GA** Waiver of Liability statement signed by the patient is in file.

**-GB** Distinct Procedural Service: This may represent a different or separate session, different procedure or surgery, different size, separate lesion, or separate injury.

Use to give further information about the service than that which is defined by the CPT code.

## CORRECT CODING INITIATIVE

Bundled services started in January 1996; this listing represents "unbundled codes" (codes that are a component of a more extensive code) and "mutually exclusive" codes combinations. Mutually exclusive codes are defined as services that by CPT definition cannot reasonably be performed at the same surgical session, by the same physician, and or on the same patient.

## CODING BULLETS

### Why is it important to code correctly?

- The physician's practice receives the **maximum legal reimbursement** for the physician services.
- The medical staff is more **efficient.**
- Reduced exposure to **fraud and abuse.**

### What is the physician's role in coding?

- The **physician should be choosing the levels of CPT coding**, not the staff.
- Physicians should be using the **full spectrum of** Evaluation and Management codes for office visits, consultations, etc.
- **Documentation** must justify the coding level.
- Self-audit of charts to verify correct coding.
- Ensure the staff is current and up to date on all coding requirements.

### Common Coding Errors

- Using consultation and office visit codes inappropriately, resulting in "down coding."
- Improper use of levels of service when billing for office, nursing home and

hospital visits without proper supporting documentation.

- Double diagnosis problems and concurrent care.
- Incorrect charges for multiple procedures.
- Improper billing of purchased diagnostic tests.
- Improper billing for supplies on Medicare/Medicaid claims.
- Failing to utilize modifiers correctly.
- Chronic use of the unlisted procedure codes.
- Failing to match diagnosis to procedure performed.
- Failing to update codes annually and stay abreast of all coding changes.

Chapter 5

# Employee Physician Contracts

*The Employee Physician Contract is a valuable tool you can use in exiting your practice and the new ophthalmologist can use toward the buy-in of the practice.*

In an employee physician relationship, the contract is one of the most important documents. This will guarantee an understanding of the expectations of the employee of the terms of employment with the practice. With your signature on the contract, the physician accepts employment and agrees to provide high quality professional ophthalmic services to the patients of the employer.

The terms of the employment agreement should include whether the ophthalmologist is to be part time or full time as well as if the physician is to work exclusively for the practice. The standards of the practice should be outlined as policy and regulations of the employer.

Items that need to be outlined include: What will the compensation be? Will health, life or disability insurance be offered? Will CME expenses be paid? Look over the terms for termination or disqualification. There are several critical points that should always be considered when preparing or reviewing employee physician contracts.

- Always get an attorney involved to draft the documents.
- Have the buy-in methodology outlined in the contract
    - What will it cost?
    - How long will it take?

## Items That Should Be Covered in the Contract:

- Employment information
- Terms and conditions
- Duties

- Compensation
- Annual salary parameters are $110,000-$125,000
- Bonus configured at 3 times salary and then $.30 on every additional $1.00
- Employee benefits
- Buy-in model and appraisal value—these both need to be affordable for the physician buying-in and yet have the ability to make the owner money
- Vacation should be two weeks the first year and three weeks the second year
- One week CME time should be given
- Moving expenses should be forgiven if the contract is fulfilled
- Buy-in should take place in year three
- It should be understood that the employee has contributed to the practice during his/her term as an employee
- Tangible assets to determine value are determined three ways:
    - Origination cost
    - Replacement cost
    - Fair market value
- The exit strategy for the owner should take five to seven years to complete
- Buy-in methodology should be utilized as the buy-out methodology
- There should always be a buy-back provision in the contract.
- Reasons for termination:
    - Death—there should be insurance to cover the remainder of the buy-out to the owner.
    - Disability—there should be insurance to cover the remainder of the buy-out. You should have a buy-back provision to cover the seller. Have all scenarios covered for the unexpected occurrences.
    - Document everything.
- Have a non-solicitation clause in the contract
- Outline the restrictive covenant, the mileage therein and the cost
- Buy-in should begin in month 25
- Have a non-compete clause—you don't want to train the competition
- So the senior partner doesn't lose control, you should have a senior protection income distribution model:

- 10% for senior protection
    - 40% equal distribution
    - 50% for productivity
- Expenses could be divided:
    - Fixed at 50% each
    - Variable
    - Percentage based on productivity
- The senior partner does not want to lose his or her decision-making ability
- What are your company standards? Where are you currently with Medicare and Medicaid? What record-keeping mechanism are you using?
- Incentives should not be 2-2.5:1. They must be 3:1.
- Remember, some physicians don't want to be owners. If your ultimate goal is to exit, you need to find a candidate who does want to be an owner.
- The terms and conditions and tax ramifications are more important than the price consideration.
- Buyers want an asset deal—Sellers will want a stock deal. All contracts require negotiations by both parties.
- Make sure your rights are covered, by getting everything in writing, and then there will be no misunderstanding or miscommunication.

Remember, the Employee Physician Contract is not infinite. It is a valuable tool that you can use as you move forward in exiting your practice and as the new ophthalmologist looks toward buy-in of a practice. It is much easier to cover every possible aspect of a buy-in/buy-out now than to try to deal with critical issues after the fact.

If you are looking to bring an ophthalmologist into your practice, you need to develop a contract. Consult with your attorney to discuss and review these contractual agreements

Young ophthalmologists coming out of school with heavy student loans focus first on compensation. We suggest they take some of the risk as well. Why pay them $120,000, $140,000 or $150,000 at the outset? Offer them $100,000 to $110,000, and then have them share the risk by going on an incentive or bonus program. This approach doesn't always work, but it is a recommended initial bargaining strategy.

Our firm recommends you try to negotiate salary at about $108,000 to $112,000 with a bonus incentive at a 3:1 ratio above the fees that you and your young ophthalmologist generate. So in fact, if you are generating 3:1 of your cost, you add your salary and your benefits. As an example, let's say it is $150,000 for the first year contract. You start your bonus incentive at $450,000, simply because you deduct your overhead and then salary and benefits, finding that all of a sudden you have no rate of return or return on your investment. In this case, you need to renegotiate, with the goal to reach up to 10% return on your investment, if at all possible.

On the other hand, you have to work with that young ophthalmologist. He or she may have student loans that have created a great deal of debt. Employment agreements are negotiable. Maybe the young physician is at a firm in Miami and you want to move him to New Orleans. Pay the moving expenses, with a ceiling, and lower the salary, so you are saving on the employer tax match.

You are also challenged by non-solicitation and restrictive covenants. Make sure that you are using an attorney familiar with the health care industry. Consider involving a third party, whether it is your accountant, your attorney or other consultant to help you negotiate the deal.

Once the young ophthalmologist has joined the practice and he or she has worked for six months to a year, you might hear, "I've worked hard and brought value to the corporation. Don't lay a $17 million price tag on me to buy-in." There is validity behind that thinking because the most important issue to the ophthalmologist buying-in is affordability. If your prospective buyer can't pay for it, the deal will fall through. Be sure you are utilizing a contract that ensures the value for buy-in and buy-out is complete.

When is it appropriate to hire an ophthalmologist? We usually suggest that if you can't afford to pay one year's salary, you can't afford to bring in an ophthalmologist. It doesn't matter if you're booked out for six months. By reviewing hundreds of ophthalmic practices, we have found that you typically need to concede up to 25% of your practice to build the new ophthalmologist's practice

What you get by hiring an ophthalmologist who will buy in is more time off. Financially, you bring an ophthalmologist in when you can afford one. In the case of a total buy-in, in which you hand over your practice, be sure to get a check to cover the sale on day one. There are also some physicians who only want to be employees—not owners. This arrangement can have advantages too, since practices will always need employee ophthalmologists.

When you are looking at actual employment agreement sections, from the economic standpoint, ask your attorney to make sure you have all duties and employment defined. The recommended term of employment is two years. In Chapter 6, we've covered the compensation level from year one to year two with the buy-in/buy-out clause configured in that arena. Make sure it is in the contract.

Employment duties need to be outlined as well. If you want ophthalmologists you hire to always take calls from now on, you need to write that in your duties format. Every duty you expect them to do should be listed. Do you expect them to work on Saturday mornings, run the optical, handle the on-call schedule, emergency calls, etc.? As an owner and the senior physician, you probably don't want to do some of those things any more, which is partly why you bring an ophthalmologist into your practice.

## Restrictive Covenants

A restrictive covenant is usually part of any employee physician contract. In ophthalmology, a median range geographically is fifty-five miles, but you can't make a geographic restrictive covenant of only fifty-five miles. Therefore, non-solicitation agreements are recommended, meaning that you will not solicit charts, patients or staff from another practice. It is advisable to check local statutes with your legal counsel. In addition to a restrictive covenant and non-solicitation agreement, your contract should cover damage solutions. We usually recommend $250,000, but you may need to adjust the amount to fit your geographic location. It needs to be a significant enough amount to make the ophthalmologist coming in think about it. Young ophthalmologists will want to work things out, they want it to be affordable, and they want to be with you forever.

## Payments to Employees After Termination

In paying employees after termination, what is your payment scheme and how do you pay them? Is it severance or buy-out? What do you call it? What is the rationale for the termination? Is it lack of performance, unethical actions or poor quality work—all of which are valid reasons? What are you going to do if you terminate them and in the ensuing months thereafter? Are you going to pay them for three months? Many ophthalmologists pay through the end of the contract, but why do they do that when they have reasons for termination?

## Employee Benefits

You really should pay as many benefits for your employees as you can. You should pay profit sharing, health care, dental and eye glasses, anything that doesn't include payroll matching to the government. Convince your staff and your doctors how valuable a profit sharing program is and how valuable health care benefits are. These are all expenses to the corporation, but not like matching 25% to the government.

## Conditions During Employment

There are several conditions that should be addressed. How do you deal with patient records? There should be a clause in the contract in the event Medicare audits you. If this happens, whose fault is it? If you are the owner of the corporation and you have an employee physician come in who cannot tell one code from another and who can't write legibly in the chart, he or she could get you caught in a fraud case. Who pays for that? Who's liable? You are. Make sure you have a clause in your contract addressing Medicare/ Medicaid fraud. Be sure to follow the law and check with your attorney for appropriate wording.

## Facilities and Work Schedule

Are you going to sell your real estate? What are your expectations relative to the facilities? If you have a three-lane practice, what days are employees expected to work? Do you want them there on Saturday mornings? Do you want them there Monday night until 7:00 p.m.? These are items that must be stipulated in the contract.

## Buy-Back

Make sure you have a buy-back provision in the contract so you can get your practice back, should the need arise. The fact is that people do die unexpectedly; some become disabled and others run away for the wildest reasons. Secure a buy-back provision so you can retrieve your practice.

## Other Considerations

Are you going to pay for malpractice insurance? Is it going to be tail insurance, or will it be based on claims made? What are you going to pay for continuing education? Are you paying for employees to attend any conferences? Do you pay for their hotel stay during the conference, or do you pay for one needing to commute? Usually a contract will have a $2,500 ceiling on CMEs. Do staff members want to go to one major, more expensive conference or several smaller conferences closer to home with less travel cost? It is the employees' choice, but when they hit the ceiling of $2,500 for tuition, for hotel, for expenses, etc., additional expenses become their own responsibility.

Are you going to pay for the ophthalmologist to relocate? I have seen contracts fail because the senior doctor would not pay $1,500 to move someone from Baltimore to Indianapolis, which is really good corporate expense. If you are so concerned, however, list those items and offer to forgive the expense after two years. Then, if he or she doesn't stay for the full term of the contract, the money must be reimbursed to you.

The average first-year contract has one week of sick leave and two weeks of vacation. The second year has three weeks of vacation, $2,500 for CMEs as mentioned before and five days of sick leave. At that point, you can move into paying certain licensures, as well as local medical society fees, state society fees and anything else you want to include.

## Ownership Rights

When are you going to let a younger ophthalmologist become the owner? Beginning in year three, how would he or she pay for it and at what price? Will there be deferred compensation? You should know what that is. Say the ophthalmologist produces $500,000 the first year and $600,000 the next year, but you only give credit for $500,000, because you transfer $100,000 to the senior doctor—yourself—as deferred compensation. After five years, he or she will have paid a half-million dollars, which constitutes the buy-in. However, as discussed in Chapter 6, when there's a buy-in there has to be a buy-out. For a million dollar practice, after paying $500,000 towards the buy-in and another $500,000 for the buy-out, you are gone and the employee physician owns it all. That's one mechanism.

In a corporate structure, you as a seller would want a future owner to buy stock, wouldn't you? If you are in a sole proprietorship, you're "cooked" because you are subject to ordinary income taxation. If you were the buyer, you would want to buy depreciable assets, although you will not enjoy the stock advantage. This can become a hot negotiating item. You might prefer a blend of an asset and a stock purchase agreement. As for assets, the young ophthalmologist will want to look at depreciated book value because that means the assets have been depreciated and cost little. We won't get into replacement versus origination cost versus depreciated book value here, but you have to sell at fair market value. Assets for a big ophthalmic corporation amount to 30-40% of the value. If you have an appraiser evaluate the fair market value, the IRS can't touch you, and according to Stark's law, it is truly the fair market value.

## Summary

To summarize, employee physician negotiations must be recorded in writing. You have to do everything in advance and complete an appraisal, which you probably should have certified. Have a licensed appraiser do your appraisal. Don't try to negotiate your own deal, and read the contract thoroughly before signing to make sure it's in your best interest. Remember, a contract is not for forever, although it may seem so at times. In a contract, make sure everything is included: a minimum two-year employment agreement, salary and bonuses. Make sure you structure and deal with the issue of the buy-in and buy-out model at this time. Leave no questions as to how this model will work.

## Some of the key points to remember include:

**CONTRACT CONTENTS:**

I. Employment

II. Term

III. Duties

IV. Compensation

  A. Annual salary

  B. Bonus

  C. Corporate benefits (i.e. insurance, pension)

  D. Buy-in model

V. Vacation

VI. Disability

VII. Termination

  A. Death

  B. Disability of 180 days

  C. Permanent disability

  D. Conviction of a felony or any crime

  E. "At Will"

  F. No solicitation of corporation patients

VIII. Non-competition

IX. Education

X. Applicable law

XI. Specific performance

XII. Binding effect

At the end of this chapter is a sample Employee Contract for your review. Please remember that contracts are individual to your practice, your philosophy, your candidate and your situation. Always seek professional advice and check with your legal and health care consultants relative to the pertinent issues that should be included for your protection.

## Sample Employment Agreement

THIS EMPLOYMENT AGREEMENT (the "Agreement") is made and entered into as of (although not necessarily on) the __________day of ________________, 20___, by and between ________________________________ an ____________ corporation, with its principal place of business at ______________________________ ______, (called "Employer"), and _______________, an individual, presently residing at __________________________(called "Employee").

WHEREAS, Employer is a medical corporation, organized under _____________ law; and

WHEREAS, Employer conducts professional services in the field of eye care and ophthalmology; and

WHEREAS, Employer interacts with related entities to provide various marketing techniques and methods to attract patients to utilize the services of Employer and related entities; and

WHEREAS, Employer desires to employ various individuals qualified to render eye care services to the patients of Employer at Employer's various locations, but also desires, among other things, to protect and preserve from disclosure or from unauthorized use the various marketing techniques and methods provided by Employer to attract patients to utilize the services of Employer; and

WHEREAS, Employee is a doctor of medicine, duly licensed (or will be) as an ophthalmologist under the laws of the State of ___________, who will as promptly as practicable obtain a license to practice medicine as an ophthalmologist under the laws of the State of ______and ___________ (the "Medical License"); and

WHEREAS, Employer desires to employ Employee, subject to the terms of this Agreement, in his capacity as an ophthalmologist; and,

NOW, THEREFORE, in consideration of the employment of Employee by Employer and the mutual agreements contained herein, it is agreed by Employee and Employer as follows:

Section 1. Employment and Duties. Employer hereby employs Employee, and Employee hereby accepts employment by Employer, as an employee on the staff of Employer, for the purpose of rendering ophthalmological medical and surgical services, to the patients of Employer, and in the manner and to the extent permitted by law and the applicable canons of professional ethics. Employee's duties, in addition to rendering the aforementioned ophthalmological services to patients of Employer, shall include, but not be limited to, the following:

(a) Keeping and maintaining, or causing to be kept and maintained, appropriate records, reports, claims, correspondence, etc. necessary and appropriate in connection with all professional services rendered by Employee under this Agreement to the patients of Employer, all of which records, reports, claims, correspondence, etc. shall belong to and be the property of Employer;

(b) Promoting, to the extent permitted by law and the applicable canons of professional ethics, the eye care services of Employer;

(c) Performing all acts reasonably necessary to maintain and improve Employee's professional skills;

(d) Provide services offsite;

(e) Cover "on-call" responsibilities during Dr. ____________absence, in addition to Employee's regular rotation;

(f) Be responsible for MD/OD consultations; and

(g) All other lawful acts relating to ophthalmology and the other eye care services of Employer as directed from time to time by Employer.

Employee's other duties shall be as the Board of Directors of Employer may from time to time reasonably direct, including on-duty and on-call assignments at night and on weekends and holidays. Such assignments shall be rotated among the employees of Employer in a reasonable manner.

Notwithstanding the foregoing provisions of this Section 1, as a condition to Employee being employed by Employer, Employee shall first (a) obtain the ___________ and ______________ Medical License; (b) acquire hospital privileges at ________________ _________________; and (c) obtain a Medicare provider number.

Further, after Employee is employed by Employer, Employee agrees to become board certified by the American Board of Ophthalmology within _____ years of employment date.

Section 2. Term of Employment. Employer employs Employee, and Employee accepts employment under the terms of this Agreement with Employer, for a period of ______________to begin _______________ (the "Initial Term"); the employment of Employee by Employer shall continue for an additional __________________period beyond the Initial Term (the Subsequent Term").

During any Subsequent Term, except as hereinafter provided, all of the terms and conditions of this Agreement applicable to the Initial Term shall apply so that the employment relationship between Employee and Employer shall continue, subject to the terms and conditions of this Agreement, for the Subsequent Term and any additional terms of___________________unless written notice of an intent not to continue the employment relationship is given by one party to the other at least _______ days before the expiration of any such additional _____________ term. Notwithstanding the ___________term, the employment of Employee by Employer may be terminated prior to expiration of the initial term or any Subsequent Term, as the case may be, pursuant to the provisions of Section 4.

Section 3. Compensation. As compensation for services rendered to Employer under the terms of this Agreement, Employee shall receive compensation as follows:

(a) Signing Bonus and Basic Salary. A signing bonus in the amount of _______________, less normal withholdings, shall be paid to Employee within

________ days of the signing of this Agreement. However, if Employee terminates his employment within ____________________ of the beginning employment date, Employee agrees to repay said __________________ to Employer at the time his employment terminates. While employed by Employer, Employee shall be paid an annual salary of ___________________ in year one, ___________ in year two, payable at least monthly.

(b) Incentive Bonus. Further, Employee shall be paid an incentive bonus in year ___ of ________ of the excess of gross collections over _____________. This bonus, if earned, will be payable within ______ days of the end of the month in which the target is exceeded and subsequent months thereafter.

Further, Employee shall be paid an incentive bonus in year ___ of ___________ of the excess of gross collections over _____________. This bonus, if earned, will be payable within ________ days of the end of the month in which the target is exceeded and subsequent months thereafter.

This incentive bonus shall be computed on Employee's _____ and _______ years of employment as opposed to computing it on a calendar year basis; although the parties agree at some point to negotiate in good faith to convert this computation so that it will be done on a calendar year basis thereafter.

Anything in this Section 3(b) to the contrary notwithstanding, if the employment of Employee is terminated pursuant to Section 4(a) (1), (2), (4), (5), (6), (7), (8), (9), or (10), Employee shall not be entitled to any Bonus with respect to the calendar year in which such termination occurs, or with respect to any calendar year thereafter.

Anything in this Section 3 to the contrary notwithstanding, Employee shall not be entitled to receive any compensation under this Agreement until Employee has first obtained the _________________ Medical License.

Section 4. Termination. The following provisions shall relate to the termination of Employee's employment with Employer:

(a) Basis for Termination. Anything in Section 2 to the contrary notwithstanding, the employment of Employee by Employer shall terminate upon the occurrence of any one of the following events:

(1) if Employee's license to practice as an ophthalmologist in the State of _____________ or ____________ is, for any reason, not renewed or is, for any reason, suspended, revoked or canceled;

(2) if there comes a time that Employee, for any reason, is disqualified to practice as an ophthalmologist under the laws of the State of ___________ or _____________ or otherwise ceases to be a "licensed person" as defined under _____________ law or _____________ law;

(3) if Employee and Employer shall mutually agree to termination in writing;

(4) the "Total Disability" (defined to mean the inability of Employee arising out of

any medically determinable physical or mental impairment to perform any of the services required by him by Employer under the terms of this Agreement) of Employee for a period of _____________ consecutive calendar days or the death of Employee;

(5) if Employee fails or refuses to perform faithfully and diligently the usual and customary duties of the employment and to comply with the provisions of this Agreement;

(6) if Employee fails or refuses to comply with the reasonable policies, standards and regulations of Employer as may be established by the Board of Directors of Employer from time to time;

(7) if Employee is found guilty of unprofessional conduct by any board, institution, organization or professional association having a privilege or right to pass upon the professional conduct of Employee;

(8) if it is determined by the Board of Directors of Employer that the use of any legally obtained drug, controlled substance, or alcohol used by Employee adversely affects Employee's job performance;

(9) if Employee is found by the Board of Directors of Employer to be engaged in the manufacturer, distribution, dispensation, sale, purchase, transfer, use or possession of illegal drugs and/or controlled substances;

(10) if Employee, upon the reasonable belief of Employer, has committed a dishonest act against Employer or any of the employees of Employer, regardless of whether such act is punishable as a criminal offense under law;

(11) by either Employer or Employee providing the other with a ____________________ day written notice of termination of this Agreement for any reason or no reason.

(b) Payments to Employee after Termination. If the employment of Employee by Employer is terminated under any of the provisions of Section (4)(a), excepting Section 4(a) (3), Employee shall be entitled to receive only that portion of the Basic Salary accrued but unpaid as of the date of termination.

Section 5. Employee Benefits. During the term of employment, Employee shall be entitled to the following benefits:

(a) Employer will pay premiums for Employee's family health insurance (carrier to be selected by Employer), with the premiums not to exceed ____________________ annually.

(b) Employer will pay premiums for Employee's disability insurance (carrier to be selected by Employer), with the premiums not to exceed ____________________ annually.

(c) Employer will pay Employee's professional liability (carrier to be selected by

Employer) premium for year one not to exceed ________________, and for year two not to exceed ______________.

(d) Employee will have a CME allowance not to exceed ______________, and a moving allowance not to exceed ________________.

(e) In the first year of employment, Employee will be entitled to ________ full working days of vacation and in year two, ___________ full working days of vacation.

(f) Employee will be permitted full _______ working days annually for CME seminars.

Section 6. Conditions During Employment. The following conditions shall apply with respect to the employment of Employee by Employer:

(a) Patient Records. All records, case histories, x-ray films, test results or personal or regular files concerning patients of Employer or patients consulted, interviewed, or treated or cared for by Employee (the "Patient Records") shall belong to and remain the property of Employer.

(b) Facilities. Employer shall provide and maintain, or cause to be provided and maintained, such facilities, equipment and supplies, as it deems necessary for the performance by Employee of Employee's professional duties as an ophthalmologist under this Agreement.

(c) Loyalty. Employee shall devote Employee's full time and best efforts to the performance of duties required under this Agreement. During the term of this Agreement, Employee shall not engage in the practice of rendering ophthalmological medical or surgical services to any extent except for the benefit of and on behalf of Employer, pursuant to and under the terms of this Agreement, and all fees and other income attributable to Employee's ophthalmological medical or surgical services performed for Employer during the term of this Agreement shall belong to Employer.

(d) Malpractice. Employee shall hold harmless and indemnify Employer, its successors and assigns, against all liabilities, costs, damages, expenses and attorney's fees (collectively referred to as the "Losses") resulting from or attributable to any act, error, omission, negligence, incompetence or malfeasance, etc. of Employee while employed by Employer that result from Employee's rendering of ophthalmological, medical or surgical services (collectively referred to as the "Risks"); provided, however, to the extent that any such Losses are compensated by insurance purchased and maintained by Employer, Employee shall not be required to reimburse Employer. In this regard, Employer shall use its best efforts to acquire and maintain professional liability insurance on a claims-made basis ("Malpractice Insurance") insuring against a claim made during Employee's employment with Employer with respect to the Risks, such insurance should be in an amount equal to $1,000,000 per occurrence and $3,000,000 in the aggregate. Upon termination of this Agreement, Employer shall have no obligation to maintain the Malpractice Insurance. If, at the date of the termination of Employee's employment with Employer, Employee has been employed by Employer for more than two (2) years or less, Employer shall use its best efforts to acquire and maintain a policy of professional liability insurance, in an amount equal to $1,000,000 per occurrence and $3,000,000 in the aggregate, insuring against any of the risks for which a claim is made at any time within the five-year period following the termination of Employee's employment under this Agreement (the "Post-Employment Malpractice Insurance"). If, at the date of the termination of Employee's employment with Employer, Employee has been employed by Employer for two (2) years or less, Employee or the legal representative of Employee's estate, as the case may be, shall acquire and maintain the Post-Employment Malpractice Insurance, which Post-Employment Malpractice Insurance shall be subject to the prior written approval of Employer; and, Employer shall reimburse Employee for one-half of the cost of acquiring and maintaining such Post-Employment Malpractice Insurance. With respect to the Post-Employment Malpractice acquired and maintained by Employee, Employee shall provide Employer with such proof of compliance and proof of premium payment as Employer may reasonably request. Employer shall have no obligation to obtain professional liability insurance with respect to any act, error, omission, negligence, incompetence or malfeasance, etc. of Employee that occurred at any time prior to Employee commencing employment with Employer.

(e) Continuing Education. Employee is encouraged and expected to attend meetings, professional conventions, postgraduate courses and seminars and other educational meetings relative to the practice of ophthalmology at reasonable times and as approved by Employer. ____ full working days of paid leave will be set aside for this purpose (these ____ full working days are the same ____ full working days referred to in Paragraph 5(f)). Subject to written approval by Employer and compliance with the Employer's policies, Employee shall be reimbursed for continuing education expenses (including the costs of medical journals, books, etc.) up to a maximum amount of _______ for the Initial term and up to a maximum of _______ for each Subsequent Term. (This ______ is the same ________ referred to in paragraph 5(d)).

(f) Sick Leave. Employee shall be entitled to ______ full working days sick leave and _____ personal full working days, annually, all as provided in the Employee Policy Manual.

(g) Licenses. The costs and expenses of Employee to initially obtain and maintain the _____________ and __________ Medical License or any prerequisites to practice in ___________ or _____________, shall be the sole costs and expenses of Employee.

(h) To the extent that any provisions of the preceding paragraphs conflict with the provisions of Section 5, the provisions in section 5 shall be controlling.

Section 7. Restricted Activity. Employee acknowledges that Employer utilizes various marketing techniques and methods to attract patients to use the services of Employer and in connection therewith, Employer has developed and maintained patient lists, files, etc. that constitute trade secrets (the "Trade Secrets") and has and maintains various information and records that, while not necessarily constituting trade secrets, are, nevertheless, confidential. Therefore, as a condition to Employer employing Employee, Employee agrees and warrants that from and after the effective date of this Agreement, unless authorized by Employer in writing, Employee will not in any manner whatsoever, directly or indirectly, as an employee, agent partner, sole proprietor, stockholder, director, consultant or otherwise, disclose to any person, firm, partnership, corporation, etc., other than an authorized agent of Employer, any of the Trade Secrets or any confidential information, records or documents relating to the patients or the business of Employer. Further, from the effective date hereof until the termination of Employee's employment with Employer, Employee agrees and warrants that Employee will not in any way, directly or indirectly, as an employee, agent, partner, sole proprietor, stockholder, director, consultant or otherwise engage in any activity (the "Restricted Activity") that is damaging, detrimental or reasonably anticipated to damage or to be detrimental to the business or operations of Employer in the "Employer Market Area" (as hereinafter defined) or of any of the physicians employed by Employer in the Employer Market Area, including, but not limited to, the following activities;

(a) diverting, taking away or attempting to take away any person that has been or is a patient of Employer or of any physician employed by Employer;

(b) soliciting, procuring, recommending or suggesting by inference or otherwise, to any person, firm, partnership, corporation, etc. that any services of the type provided by Employer or any of the physicians employed by Employer be obtained from any other physician, entity or entities; or

c) diverting from Employer or attempting to divert or take away from Employer any person who is an employee or prospective employee of Employer.

Further, unless such restriction is otherwise prohibited by law, Employee agrees that until the expiration of _______ years following the date of termination of Employee's employment by Employer, Employee will not engage in the Restricted Activity in the Employer Market Area. Additionally, from the effective date hereof until ________years following the termination of Employee's employment with Employer, Employee agrees and warrants that Employee will not in any way engage as an employee, agent, partner, sole proprietor, stockholder, director, consultant or in any other capacity in any business or enterprise, the nature of which is competitive to the business of Employer, or of any of the physicians employed by Employer in the Employer Market Area. As used in this Section 7, "Employer Market Area" includes the following:

(a) the geographic areas within a ___ mile radius of Employer's main office facilities,

(b) all area within the city limits of _______________, and

(c) the geographic areas within a ____ mile radius of any additional satellite offices of Employer opened for business during the period that Employee is employed by Employer.

In the context of the foregoing provisions of this Section 7, if a reasonable question arises as to whether an activity is prohibited or whether it is permitted and reasonable minds would differ in the resolution of such question, it shall be presumed that such activity is an activity that is prohibited.

If the Employee violates the preceding provision, Employee shall immediately pay Employer on demand as liquidated damages, in addition to any other damage or remedy due Employer, the sum of _________ per month, or any part thereof for as long as the violation continues. The parties also agree that Employer shall suffer irreparable damage if this provision is not specifically enforced. If any dispute arises concerning the application of this provision, the parties agree an injunction may be issued restraining activities by Employee pending the termination of such dispute. Any such dispute and the rights of Employer in relation thereto shall be enforceable in a court of equity by a decree of specific performance and such remedy shall be cumulative and not exclusive and in addition to any other remedy which Employer may enjoy. Employee acknowledges that the foregoing provisions of this paragraph are reasonable and necessary and in view of the unique nature of Employer and its medical operations and in view of unique and confidential information which will necessarily be made available to Employee by Employer. Employee shall also pay any reasonable attorneys' fees incurred by Employer to enforce its rights under this paragraph or this Agreement.

Section 8. Ownership Rights. Employee agrees that any files, lists and/or directories made by Employee during the term of Employee's employment, solely or jointly with others or with Employer's equipment, supplies, facilities or time, or which relate to the business of Employer or Employer's actual or anticipated patient development, or which result from any work performed by Employee for Employer shall be the exclusive property of Employer or its designee shall have the right to keep and possess all such items. Employee agrees that Employee will promptly and fully inform and disclose to Employer all such files, lists, directories, designs, improvements and/or discoveries.

Section 9. Court Actions. Inasmuch as the damages which Employer or the Related Entities would sustain by reason of the breach by Employee of any of the provisions of this Agreement would be difficult if not impossible of ascertainment, Employer shall be entitled to enjoin any continuing violation of this Agreement and may apply to any court having jurisdiction for a temporary restraining order and an injunction to restrain and enjoin any further violation of this Agreement. In this regard, Employee specifically agrees (i) that if any litigation should arise between Employer and Employee with regard to this Agreement, Employee shall submit to the jurisdiction and venue of the state and federal courts located in ________________________, and (ii) that a temporary injunction may be entered in such litigation preventing disclosure of any matters regarding this Agreement during the pendency of such litigation.

Section 10. Purchase Into Practice. A reasonable time after completion of ___ months of mutually satisfactory employment of Employee by Employer, Employee shall be eligible to be elected as a potential stockholder of Employer. If Employee is elected as a potential stockholder of Employer by the unanimous consent of the then existing stockholders of Employer, Employee shall be entitled to purchase shares of stock of Employer. Any shares of stock in Employer purchased by Employee shall be purchased pursuant to a Stock Purchase Agreement executed by Employee and Employer substantially the same as that set forth as Exhibit "B" attached hereto and made a part hereof for all purposes (the "Stock Purchase Agreement"); and, the effective date of the Stock Purchase Agreement so executed shall be when Employee becomes a potential stockholder of Employer.

Section 11. Notices. Any notice or other communication to any party pursuant hereto shall be deemed to have been given or delivered when deposited in the United States Mail, registered or certified, and with proper registration or certification fee prepaid, addressed to the party for whom intended, as follows:

| To Employer: | To Employee: |
|---|---|
| ______________________________ | ______________________________ |
| ______________________________ | ______________________________ |

or to such other address as the party to be given such notice may designate by written notice to the other party in the manner hereinbefore provided.

Section 12. Employee to Provide Automobile. Employee agrees to furnish a properly registered automobile for all transportation needs required for the performance of Employee's duties under this Agreement. At all times during the term of Employee's employment, Employee shall keep in full force and effect at Employee's sole expense automobile insurance on each such automobile owned by employee that is used at any time to carry out any of the duties of employment. Each such policy must be issued by an insurance company acceptable to Employer and must include the name of Employer as a named insured. Each such policy shall insure against public liability for bodily injury in the minimum amount of _____________ per person and ____________ per occurrence and for property damage in the minimum amount of ______________. Employee shall deliver a certificate for each such policy to Employer.

Section 13. Binding Agreement. This Agreement shall be binding upon Employee and shall inure to the benefit of Employer, and the provisions hereof shall survive any termination of this Agreement by either party. Further, this Agreement shall be binding upon and inure to the benefit of the parties hereto and their respective heirs, successors and assigns.

Section 14. Indemnification. Employee hereby indemnifies Employer against any and all actions, suits, claims, demands or prosecutions that may be brought or instituted against Employer as a result of the acts of Employee that are in violation of this Agreement, and also against all damages, costs and expense, including attorneys' fees that Employer may pay, incur or become liable for in defending or compromising the same.

Section 15. Governing Law. This Agreement shall be interpreted and construed under the laws of the State of ________________________. If Employee shall breach this Agreement in whole or in part, Employee shall pay Employer's reasonable attorneys' fees, court costs and other expenses incurred by Employer in enforcing this Agreement.

Section 16. Waiver. No waiver of any breach or default hereunder shall be deemed or construed to constitute a waiver of any other breach or default hereunder, and forbearance to enforce one or more of the remedies herein provided or otherwise available upon any breach or default shall not be deemed or construed to constitute a waiver of such breach or default.

Section 17. Contractual Nature. The terms of this Agreement are contractual, and each and every Section is a material inducement without which this Agreement would not have been entered into by Employer.

Section 18. Rules of Construction. Titles and headings to the various sections of this Agreement are utilized as a matter of convenience only and shall not control or affect the meaning or construction of any of the terms or provisions herein.

Section 19. Counterpart and Multiple Original Execution. This Agreement may be executed in multiple counterparts, each of which shall constitute an original. This Agreement may be executed in multiple originals, each of which shall constitute a valid original.

Section 20. Authority. Any of the provisions of this Agreement required to be approved by the Board of Directors of Employer have been approved and authorized.

Section 21. Survival Provisions. In case any one or more of the provisions contained in this Agreement shall for any reason be held to be invalid, illegal, or unenforceable in any respect, such invalidity, illegality, or unenforceability shall not affect any other provision, and to the extent possible such invalid, illegal or unenforceable provision shall be reformed in a form so that it is not invalid, illegal or unenforceable; however, if such invalid, illegal or unenforceable provision cannot be so reformed in such a manner so that it is not invalid, illegal or unenforceable, then this Agreement shall be construed as if such invalid, illegal or unenforceable provision had never been included in the Agreement.

Section 22. Entirety and Amendments. This instrument and any instruments referred to herein embody the entire agreement between the parties, supersede all prior agreements and understandings, if any, relating to the subject matter hereof, and may be amended only by an instrument in writing executed by all parties, and supplemented only by documents delivered or to be delivered in accordance with the express terms hereof.

IN WITNESS WHEREOF, the parties have executed this Employment Agreement as of the day and year first above written.

| Employer: | Employee: |
|---|---|
| ______________________________ | ______________________________ |
| ______________________________ | ______________________________ |

Chapter

6

# Exit Strategies: The Succession Story

*If the succession is the result of your death, and nothing is in writing, there will be trouble. Thirty days after the death of an ophthalmologist, the practice value can often drop as low as $.03 to $.07 on the dollar. You basically have a fire sale.*

In this chaotic world of practice acquisitions, mergers, equity buy-ins and buy-outs, we have found the mechanism for success. Sell the physicians, their philosophies and their abilities, not just the practice and its physical assets. You must begin with a willing buyer and a willing seller. Though this seems like a reasonable and logical premise, it is not always true. If the buyer is a hospital or a third-party carrier, remember the golden rule of reciprocity does not always apply. Those who have the gold make the rules. Physicians are the reason practices are successful, not charts, assets, bricks or mortar. If you are selling because of fear, complacency or greed, you are making a terrible mistake. Your success will be measured by days, not years, if you react in that most unfavorable manner.

Frequently, ophthalmologists call us to ask, "I want to retire tonight, tomorrow or on Sunday, but how can I accomplish that?" In the days when practice management companies would buy you out, the whole deal could be closed within 90 days. Then there were short-term options you could utilize to make this happen, but buy-outs like this don't happen today. Now the exit strategies for ophthalmologists are normally three- to seven-year programs, in which typically a younger associate will want to buy-in. First, though, he or she must agree to buy you out.

We've all heard stories of physicians dying suddenly or suffering a disabling heart attack, stroke or accident. While these sound extreme or rare, such events do happen and are out of our control. There are multiple ways to exit; some you control, such as shutting down the practice and putting a padlock on the door. Some you don't control, such as death or disability. If you currently have partners, associates or colleagues, you should know who you want to take over the practice. Make sure you put your intentions in writing, however. Be sure you have cross-purchase agreements and effective buy/sell agreements. Why? Because, if something happens to you, you want your patients to be treated and your staff to be cared for. And, what about your spouse and children? Without a written agreement, you run a dangerous risk of leaving out important details.

When an ophthalmologist dies unexpectedly, the spouse wants to know what to do next. The best plan is to liquidate, especially if there is a big mortgage to pay and three children under twenty to support. If the documents are there to cover you and a practice appraisal is done that assesses assets and future earnings potential, the surviving spouse is better prepared to look for a buyer.

You would be surprised at the number of practices where employment agreements go unsigned and there are no cross-purchase agreements. If the succession is the result of your death, and nothing is in writing, there will be trouble. Thirty days after the death of an ophthalmologist, the practice value can drop to as low as $.03 to $.07 on the dollar. You basically have a fire sale. So please, if you learn anything from this chapter, always secure the details in writing. Have the proper documents prepared and signed *before* they are needed.

## Objectives and Goals

Take time to record your objectives and goals. For instance, when do you really want to retire? There are ophthalmologists today who are 68 years young, and I mean the "young." They claim, "I'm going to retire. I'm really going to leave. I'll retire in three years." More often than not, however, they are going to work until the day they die because they love what they do. Such excellent, dedicated ophthalmologists as these should have a twelve-year exit program. So, be sure to write down your philosophy, your principles and what you really want to do.

Other ophthalmologists want a quick fix. Some physician practice management companies still exist that will consider buying a practice, but you usually need an ambulatory surgery center attached to your clinic before they'll consider it. These companies can be "quick fix" artists in some regard, not to be taken as a negative characterization. They could buy your practice and close the deal, letting you leave within three to six months, but that isn't the norm in today's world.

As mentioned earlier, one of the most important things to remember is to have your plan in writing from the beginning. Typically today, a young ophthalmologist joins you with a two-year employment agreement. Then, if he or she agrees to a buy-in, there must be a buy-out, typically a three-, five- or seven-year program. If your approach is "come sign the employment agreement and we'll figure it out in the 23rd month," you will end up in a "partnership divorce." This split occurs when in the 23rd month, you, as seller, say, "The practice is worth $17 million." The buyer retorts, "Wait, I brought a lot to the value of the practice and I should pay only $198,000." This kind of negotiation often breaks down, followed by a partnership break-up. This type of miscalculated scenario demonstrates why you need to have your exit strategy written and signed well ahead.

It is rare for anybody to plan for less than a three- to five-year exit window. I strongly advise you to lay your strategy down as soon as you can. But where do you find a buyer? You could go to your local hospital—believe it or not, some hospitals are still buying ophthalmic practices to obtain surgery patients. As long as you don't have an ambulatory surgery center, a hospital might consider buying you out. But what is the number one source of a buy-out? Whereas in the past it used to be physician practice management companies (PPMC), today it is often your competition. If you decide to approach competitive ophthalmic groups, please be sure to ask them to sign both confidentiality and non-disclosure forms to keep the discussions and ensuing transaction private. You don't want the word to get around that you are selling your ophthalmic practice.

The conversion period is usually twelve months, meaning that you, the senior ophthalmologist, the seller—are going to stay on for twelve months to convert the practice. But how should you be compensated during those twelve months, considering your reputation, capitalization and such? The typical approach would be to pay you on a percentage basis, and make you an employee of the corporation, sole proprietorship or partnership. Someone buying in to the practice should not come into the practice planning to take over immediately, unless he or she can pay for it up front.

Ophthalmologists often want to cut their hours down to one-third time. An ophthalmologist coming in must be responsible for 25% of your practice as well as building his/her own practice too. If you're just going to hand your practice over from day one, make your deal and get your money, you will have completed your buy-in and buy-out. Then you can slow down.

Of course, the primary issue for any buyer is affordability. You can argue over a price like you would for a new car, but the primary concern for the buyer is, "Can I afford it?" The next concern is how long it takes. If your buyer is a young ophthalmologist who still has student loans to pay and your practice is valued at $1 million or $500,000, how long will the buy-out take? The buyer needs to come in with eyes wide open, understanding the real costs, such as what $100,000 dollars a year at prime plus 2% interest really means in buying out a half million-dollar practice. It is interesting though, when a physician becomes an owner, the mentality changes altogether. Suddenly, as the new owner invests more energy and time into the practice, working very hard, the value seems twice what it was before.

Practice owners often ask if a buy-out should mirror the buy-in. Will today's value work for both seller and buyer at the buy-out? If the practice today is worth a million dollars, will it be worth that at buy-out time? Only 25-30% of the time does that actually occur. The caveat, though, is that if the practice buys assets over the next five years, there will be value. If there is an excess of future earnings (which is what you really value), you're not just offering goodwill, but future earnings potential. Typically you'll set a price for buy-in and then you'll follow a structure that says, "We'll then evaluate the buy-out in five years." The story is staged by what you do when you begin the process.

Our firm is often asked to help a practice to strategize an exit. We first gather all the pertinent data. We determine the physician's philosophy and goals. We review income and consider the seller's current age and plan for succession, including expectations and time frames. When dealing with a horrific disability, the window of sale is usually three months, because of the situation. The conditions are totally different in other scenarios. If looking at someone who says, "I want to be out of my practice either mentally or physically in one year," our preparation is different. If someone says, "I have a seven-year program for my exit strategy," we are operating in a more normal scenario that allows us ample time to work through ways to find interested parties who will buy-in and buy-out.

If you want to find a buyer today, look at hospitals, the competition, practice management companies or other entities. Yes, you can advertize in professional magazine or journal classified sections. While this is one way to sell your practice, and some brokers in ophthalmology will do that for you, it is usually not successful. Bulletin boards at various conferences and meetings post Practice for Sale notices, providing revenue, patient numbers and price, which does work occasionally. A doctor not long ago who wanted to buy a practice in Southeast Florida contacted our firm. We happened to know someone else who wanted to sell a practice in the same area. The two got together and worked out a deal. Less than 1% of the time this happens; it is very, very, rare.

The first decision you need to make when considering an exit is the price tag. What is the value going to be? What are the buy-in and buy-out rates rate going to be? To make these decisions, you have to conduct and review a practice evaluation, and also consider the differences between buyer and seller. The buyer wants affordable, reasonable terms and guarantees of future earnings (of course, there are no guarantees, only projections). The seller probably wants more immediacy of cash, tax management, secure care for his/her patients and staff, etc. In fact, the two parties are fundamentally different. Especially with a young ophthalmologist going through the buy-in process, you have to provide a value and data on gross income, expenses, net income and owner compensation.

How did the practice management companies handle buy-outs in their heyday? They said, "Okay, doctor, you're making $250,000. Our multiple is five, and this practice is worth $1,250,000. We want to buy half. Here is $750,000. Now the deal is done…here's your cash." The problem with that approach is that it is too simplistic. To structure your value, you have to look at both assets and cash flow.

"Goodwill" is the one word that turns everybody off in selling a practice. You might think there is no such thing as goodwill. In many states it does exist, but in most states you cannot measure personal goodwill. Check with local attorneys in your area to be sure. Only organizational goodwill can be assigned a value, which you must determine before structuring a price, taking into account cash flow and your assets. You'd love to have replacement cost or origination price for your assets, but the buyer will want depreciated book value. The same principle applies with the cash flow. Practice values in today's ophthalmology market typically are laid out at about 70-72% of the year's gross revenue. For a million dollar ophthalmic corporation, the value for everything, including assets and cash flow, would be, generically speaking, approximately $700,000. The value also depends on any existing liabilities and the age of the equipment. Real estate adds a totally different caveat to the equation.

If you were the buyer and preparing to buy-in, how much would you want to pay? Of course, you'd love to get the practice for as little as possible, wouldn't you? In that case value becomes a negotiating point. I strongly urge you to engage someone else in the negotiations besides you and the other partner. Dissention and animosity between the two doctors who are negotiating over value can be ruinous. On one side, the selling doctor sees all the value he/she has provided over the years as well as the risks taken. On the other, well, you can guess the rest of this story. Having an intermediary for the negotiations will reduce the potential for personal animosity.

But again, income and expenses aren't categories you can look at in an exit strategy for only a one-year period of time. For a truer analysis, you need to go back five years to weight income and expenses. Then you need the pro forma if you're going to sell the practice and make your exit. Pro formas are financial documents used to determine if revenue can be improved. For instance, is there room for growth in Lasik volume, coding, pricing, or other areas? Looking at the expense side and knowing that the average weighted overhead is somewhere in the 58-62% bracket for ophthalmology, we typically suggest you should realize \$.28 to \$.32 for every \$1.00 as owner compensation. These factors are all measurable, and they are vitally important in your story, because a buyer, hospital, competitor or ophthalmologist coming in wants to not only buy and share the assets, but wants to buy the ability for potential future earnings.

On average, employed ophthalmologists today make an estimated \$150,000. If they become an owner and start to buy-in on a prorated basis, they shouldn't get everything on the first day. When they can earn \$300,000, that \$150,000 has value—the ability to make an owner's wage. You take that \$150,000, multiply it by whatever capitalization you use, 4 or 5, and you have your cash flow value. That's what you need to sell.

If you have already sold your practice or bought one, you can appreciate what you are reading here. You know how necessary it is to get the right paperwork and documentation in place in order to have your practice evaluated using real numbers, and then to get all of the confidentiality agreements done, stipulating punitive damages for breaching those agreements should they talk in the doctor's lounge (and they will).

How do you structure a strategy for succession? Do you look at it internally, externally or a combination of both? You can look internally for a buy-in/buy-out. The most preferred method is by adding an ophthalmologist in your employ who will move into ownership capacity. You can always continue this succession plan by adding a third doctor into the plan. Once you are a three-doctor practice, you can then go on to doctor number four, etc. The succession story can continue on.

If you want to sell just a piece of your accounts receivable or if you want to sell on some type of productivity basis and not go through an appraisal, that's fine. Just don't sell your soul in doing this. Ophthalmologists who think they can take part of your accounts receivable as the sum of the buy-in are undervaluing your risk capitalization and twenty or thirty years of hard work. Our firm challenges people to think carefully about it.

The internal succession method in ophthalmology is the most often used method today. There aren't a lot of outside companies anymore, anyway, and it's rare for a local hospital to buy an ophthalmology practice. You may think the competition might buy you out or just wait in your parking lot for patients to come to them. That's why it becomes very difficult—they are your competition. Even if you are "friends" with your competition, are you going go talk to them yourself or hire an intermediary? It can be tricky.

For an ophthalmologist, the combination of 50:50 or 60:40 ownership is optimal, but, most young ophthalmologists cannot afford that split at the outset. Therefore, you look for them to buy maybe a third, then you sell a third externally to another ophthalmologist, a merger, the competition or a hospital, and maintain a third for yourself. If you demand a majority ownership of 50.1%, I urge you to think differently, because it doesn't make a lot of sense. You might want to sell off 25% to the physician coming up and 25% externally. In that scenario, the young ophthalmologist is not looking at a $150,000 price tag. Affordability, as stated above, it paramount the ophthalmological resident or fellow. What he/she might seek is a salary of $120,000 a year for two years with benefits, moving costs, expenses paid for a couple of conferences, and $125 towards CMEs. But, he/she most likely can't afford $700,000.

Another approach used many times is to separate the components, or entities, of your practice. For instance, if you have a clinic, ASC, optical shop or another division, they can be segmented out, lowering the price. After an evaluation, a buy-in could be just to the clinic, not the optical. The building could be removed and then added back in for the buy-in in years five through ten. Think creatively. You can segregate your business into four key components in ophthalmology—clinic, ASC, optical and building—to make them more palatable. You can become a landlord, retaining ownership as a built-in annuity. You can own the optical shop or sell the optical shop down the road to another optical shop, another OD or another MD.

You can think you're worth a million dollars all you want, but if you can't find a buyer, you are not worth a million dollars. So, you must do it correctly by IRS rules, and at fair market value. Fair market value, not blue sky, and not crazy multiples—fair market. You've also need to consider, as said before, that personal goodwill versus organizational goodwill will play into the strategy. Most ophthalmology practice owners can only sell off or classify goodwill under the IRS ruling in terms of organizational or enterprise goodwill. Personal goodwill walks out the door when you leave. It is non-salable. You should check with your local counsel on the rules for your particular geographic area.

Disability is one of the worst case scenarios for an exit. You receive $10,000 a month but you're disabled. The cleanest exit from a technical point of view is death, but disability is a realistic possibility to consider. When conducting a cross-purchase agreement, you can factor in the potential for disability by purchasing insurance to cover it. Don't wait until it's too late. Begin the idea process for your exit and document it right now, whether it will be intern, external or a combination of both. By documenting everything, you empower your intermediary to subscribe and support you in any eventuality, whether it is working with your junior partner or your competitor. With your philosophy clearly laid out and a solid business plan, negotiations are likely to be more productive and smooth. The business plan is essential not only in the development of your exit strategy, but in the development of everything you do in your clinic. As stated earlier, you should have a budget, a business plan and a structure in line that you can refer to if something happens. It will also inform your spouse about how you wanted affairs handled.

If you sell your practice, do you also want to sell your assets? Do you want to sell stock? While no rule applies universally, in general, you want to be incorporated and you want to sell stock and capital gains with some blend of ordinary income. Purchasers will usually negotiate an asset acquisition for tax management reasons. You also have to figure out how you are going to back out and be paid once your owner compensation reaches $300,000 and the employed ophthalmologist wanting to buy you out makes $150,000.

It is also good to have your income distributed across three components: productivity, equal distribution and senior protection. Productivity is great if you're the producer, but you are now backing off on your workload. With equal distribution, you all get money if you're a stockholder. The typical distribution is 60% based on productivity, 20% on equal ownership distribution and 20% based on senior protection. In senior protection, for the life of the buy-in/buy-out, the owner, the originator and/or the senior, gets 20% of all money for risk, capitalization and reward for having started the practice. A buyer would ask why, after an overhead of $400,000, a senior doctor should get $80,000 for just hanging around, but the answer is that he or she spent the money to establish the practice, The $80,000 is re-capitalization and a reward for hard work. The percentage can be modified, but the key concept here is three pools of income, not straight productivity, which is great for true producers. The physician who is a little slower, not producing as much, will like equal distribution plus a percentage, such as 1%, to go to the senior for the his/her ability to capitalize and re-tool and for starting the practice twenty or thirty years ago.

Develop a business plan document and strategy that incorporates a budget, which is as important as price is for tax strategies. Make sure you talk to your accountant about the tax side of all of your decisions, including a buy/sell agreement, cross purchase agreement and practice appraisal. Suppose someone gives you $500,000 in cash. After paying a 37% tax on it, you may wish you had instead used a deferred compensation approach or more of a stock or capital gains treatment. By lowering the price a little bit, both buyer and seller can benefit; for the one buying-in will know what the capital gains treatment will be and the seller will save $.30 on the dollar in taxes. That's pretty good for the seller too.

Most important of all considerations are the terms and conditions of the deal. What happens if the note fails? What happens during the buy-in/buy-out if one or the other partner dies? Suppose you have a two-year employment agreement, and Dr. B is going to start in year three buying-in to 50% ownership, calculated at 10% over five years on deferred compensation. What happens on the first day of the third year? In month twenty-five does Dr. B become a full 50% owner? Because it's pro rata, you shouldn't give up half of your corporation one day into the third year. Though many do give up their half this way, the buy-in should be on a pro rata basis so that by the end of year three, Dr. B holds 10%. At the end of year four, it increases to 20%, and so on each year.

When an ophthalmologist says, "I want control. I want a million dollars. I want to own 51%, and that's my exit strategy," any expert advisor will respond that 51% is not necessary. In fact, the percentage can be anything you want, although most people want equal percentages. No matter which scenario you are considering, talk to an attorney about what your rights are. If you keep it at 50:50, you can remain as the managing partner by executing a Managing Partner Agreement, to which you attach every decision that will be made of any volatile basis. You retain control this way. You can sell 50% of the practice or you can sell 10% or 13%. It doesn't really matter in terms of managing control.

It is unrealistic for the ophthalmologist/seller to expect the buy-out to be completed in two years—in cash. Today's credit lines aren't the same as they were a decade or more ago. No buyer will be able to obtain the cash, so you need to establish a program to make sure the buy-out is affordable. If you state your intention to exit, you are likely to meet with an expectation that the buyer wants to own 50% immediately and 50% upon your exit. This is the point at which you need to define how you will be compensated. You can't avoid taxes, but you can decide on a strategy that reduces your tax burden. For instance, you could be better off with $500,000 capital gains than with $1 million in an asset deal, especially later on.

When you look at your exit strategy options, weigh whether to go for a merger or acquisition. There may be advantages to you to merge rather than sell out. When two competitive groups merge, implementing a buy/sell cross purchase, the merger becomes your vehicle of exit. Have you also thought about an MD selling to an OD or vice versa? These are two other approaches you might want to consider.

Assets have three components to consider: replacement cost, origination price and depreciated book value. Carefully calculate your fair market value, including your equipment. For instance, if you bought a brand new laser, find out its current value, which is likely high, although the general rule is 52% of original cost. In contrast, if you bought an old slit lamp twenty years ago, it may be worth only $.30 on the dollar. Ophthalmic equipment holds tremendous value like in no other specialty.

This general rule will give you an idea of how valuation works: normally, a physical asset appraisal will be about 30-35% of the value. Again, if you take that million-dollar appraisal value, expect $350,000 to be assets and about $650,000, roughly, to be goodwill future earnings. These concepts drive your exit. You may wonder if today is as good a time for an exit as five years ago. That is impossible to answer. It's all relative. Today is a good day for mergers and competitive sales if you can sell to the competitors within a twelve, twenty-four or thirty-six month period or to the young ophthalmologist coming out of residency and fellowship, ready to begin buying-in, and later to buy you out.

A successful exit will occur when knowledgeable, willing buyers and sellers work together and negotiate from a fairness doctrine. By following the suggestions in this chapter, you should be equipped to realize the best possible outcome for your own exit.

Chapter 7

# Practice Appraisal Evaluations

*It has finally become apparent that a medical practice has value and, as with any service organization, there are prospective buyers who see the value.*

Over the last decade there have been many changes in the health care field. None of these is more pronounced than the appraisal for the sale of medical practices to potential buyers. It has finally become apparent that a medical practice has value and, as with any service organization, there are prospective buyers who see the value. Prospective buyers include:

- Other medical entities wanting to expand or secure markets
- Hospitals who want geographic control
- Employee doctors who want to buy-in 100% to ownership in a medical practice

The challenge in selling a practice today comes in the valuation and its methodology. History has shown there are as many ways to complete a practice valuation as there are specialties. The evaluator, no matter how objective, must use some subjectivity in this process. Most appraisers tend to use a two-pronged approach. The first phase is to assess tangible physical assets, such as buildings, furniture, and equipment, which have always had real value. The difficulty in an appraisal comes to the forefront in phase two—intangible assets—better known as goodwill.

## Estimated Value of Net Tangible Assets

In valuing the net tangible assets, the accounting method applied by the corporation must be scrutinized to determine if the market values of their tangible assets are fairly represented. The financial statements are analyzed and adjustments are made to reflect estimated market values for tangible assets and financial liabilities, and to recognize unrecorded assets and liabilities of the corporation. The primary adjustments to this cash basis are denoted as follows:

1. A prudent valuator would apply either the theorem of 50% of market replacement cost, 80% of origination cost, or book value, whichever is most reasonable, to determine the physical asset appraisal value.

2. It is reasonable to assume there would be a cash position in any corporation, as illustrated by the underlying financial statements.

3. It is fully anticipated that an offset to the accounts receivable would be reasonable. Although the accounts receivable many times will remain with the seller of an entity, in my opinion accounts receivable should be part of the tangible asset position. Therefore, accounts receivable would be valued at a normal and acceptable collection rate of 75%.

4. There are certain reasonable liability offsets that would be achieved by any practice sale that would be determined through a typical current liability scenario, along with an offset to the mortgage.

## Estimated Goodwill Value

Our firm's methodology of evaluating goodwill strives to move health care into the next century with all other service industries and make it a tangible, real asset number. We utilize three methods of evaluating goodwill:

- Excess Earnings Method
- Gross Receipts Method
- Excess Future Earnings Method

## Excess Earnings Method

This method estimates the value of goodwill based on a comparison of the earnings for the practice to that of other practices, both nationally and within the same geographic area. A corporation's earnings are usually defined as earnings before owner's salary, discretionary fringe benefits, retirement plan contributions and corporate income taxes. The earnings are analyzed based on tax returns filed with the Internal Revenue Service.

This approach involves development of weighted average earnings for the practice. The most recent years' earnings are assigned a higher weighting, based on the assumption that they more fairly represent future earnings expectations. Quite often, the valuator will weight the most recent year with a value of three, the next most recent year at a value of two, and the earliest year with a value of one. However, in certain circumstances, a heavier weighting of the most recent years might be deemed more appropriate.

## Gross Receipts Method

This method estimates the goodwill value of a practice by applying a valuation factor to the gross receipts generated by the practice. The factor value varies depending upon the type of practice under consideration. Practices with high patient retention and return rates tend to have higher factor values than surgical specialties and referral-based medical subspecialties.

In recent years past, the factor value had approached 100%, which produced a goodwill value of one year's gross receipts. However, Congress recently enacted Resource Based Relative Value Studies (RBRVS), which allows valuations to reflect the longevity of a practice, among other factors. Mature practices with long-established records of superior earnings, especially in a competitive market, tend to command higher valuation factors. Newer practices, those with average results, and those in areas with little or no real competition, will typically have lower valuation factors. Considering the age of the subject practice, office location, earnings performance and area competition, a reasonable gross receipts factor can be determined for the valuation.

## Excess Future Discounted Cash Flow Method

This method estimates the goodwill value of a practice based on the current net value of the practice's anticipated excess future earnings stream. Future earnings are estimated on the basis of either current practice earnings or a detailed forecast for future periods. A discount rate is selected based on current risk-free rates of return, plus a factor for the perception of risk involved in either achieving the forecasted results or retaining the existing income stream.

Suppose there was no detailed forecast prepared to project the anticipated future earnings stream for a practice. In this case, the adjusted earnings for the calendar year ending December 31 would be used. A reasonable rate of return and a capital recovery period that would be expected by an investor are determined, based on current mid-term rates for risk-free investments and a premium for the perceived risk of retaining the current income stream in the field. This rate and term also approximate the typical financing rate and repayment term a seller might expect to obtain if the financing was obtained from a commercial bank.

## Estimated Goodwill Value Summary

Each of the methods used to estimate the value of goodwill has support, and should be considered in determining the total estimated value for the goodwill of the practice. However, because all methods are not necessarily equally appropriate in all circumstances, the values indicated by each approach are weighted based on the perceived applicability to the practice. More weight is given to the methodology that takes into account more of the factors specifically related to the practice.

## Overall Summary

While the focus here is on the methodology used to determine the value of your practice, it is important to consider factors other than simply a dollar value. The importance of employment agreements, buy-sell agreements, stock purchase agreements and other key documents can have a dramatic impact on your practice and your current lifestyle standards. You should also be engaged in effective networking, not only for managed care, but also for determining your future and positioning yourself in the market.

In the next section of this chapter, you will see a sample Practice Appraisal Valuation. This is a very complicated process that involves careful and thorough review of all aspects of the financial areas your practice.

# Practice Appraisal Valuation Sample

## SCOPE OF THE ASSIGNMENT

The Appraiser was engaged to value the medical practice of Company X as of July 31, 2008. The focus of the valuation is the corporation, Company X. It does not include a valuation of real estate or building in which the corporation is housed. This valuation was completed to assist management in determining the asking price for the sale of an ownership interest to other licensed ophthalmologists, hospitals, and/or outside entities. It should not be used for any other purpose. It must be assumed the information provided to the Appraiser was accurate and fairly calculated. The majority of the valuation has come simply from the management reporting mechanism and the interview process. Our firm has developed and utilized this two-fold approach as the appropriate methodology for the valuation of ophthalmic practices. The valuation must stand on its own merit through the techniques utilized, as follows:

A. Interviewing process with key employees - Dr. Y, Dr. X, Mr. G, Dr. ZZ and Dr. Z.

B. A list of items prepared by management noted as follows:

- Articles of incorporation, including a notation as to the number of shares of stock issued and outstanding.
- Space agreements with landlord or any doctor.
- Any employment agreements.
- Agreement with hospital regarding the arrangement between doctors.
- Aged trial balance of accounts receivable of the practice at the end of July 31, 2008. We were most interested in the aging total (30 days, 60 days, 90 days, 120+ days).
    - o Any summary information regarding amounts due from individuals versus amounts due from third party payers.
- Accounts payable at end of July 31, 2008. If there was no accounts payable system on the computer, this may have been accumulated based on bills paid after August 1, 2008, and invoices still not paid that relate to goods or services received or provided on or before the end of July 2008. A detailed list was required, including the vendor, type of expense and the dollar amount owed at the end of July 2008.
- Unpaid profit-sharing plan contribution for 2008, if any.
- Any wages, salaries or bonuses earned as of the end of July 2008, but not paid until after that date.

- Details regarding any unpaid tax liabilities (payroll, income, sales, franchises, business, etc.) related to the corporation at the end of July 2008.
- Summarized terms of the office lease with the hospital, including the square feet, monthly rental amount, escalator provisions, renewals, and any information regarding initial rent abatements or subsidies. A copy of the lease was reviewed, if provided.
- Information concerning any equipment obligations, including installment notes payable to banks or equipment leases. For bank notes, the balance at the end of July 2008 and the payment terms were required. For equipment leases, the equipment cost and a copy of the lease agreement were needed.
- The corporate profit-sharing plan adoption agreement or other documentation identifying the type of plan and the eligibility requirements for coverage. Also, the amount contributed to the plan each year that a contribution has been made, and a separate notation of the amount contributed to the plan on behalf of Company X (if any) for each year.
- Chamber of Commerce data or other information that was available regarding the doctors including:
    - Age demographics
    - Population
    - Major industry and employers
    - Local area map indicating the location of the practice within the city and state
    - Approximate drawing radius (miles) of the practice, indicated on local area map
- Information regarding life insurance policies on the physicians, if any, including cash surrender value, annual premium, name of the insured, the beneficiary on the policy, and the policy anniversary date. This includes only those policies paid for with corporation dollars (not personal policies).
- Information about the primary competition for the practice, including:
    - Names of competing doctors
    - Location (proximity to your practice)
    - Estimate volume of competitor's practice
- Projected gross fees for the practice for 2008.
- 2000 practice budget, also 2008, if available.
- Compensation paid to doctors by the corporation through July 31, 2008, including both W-2 and 1099 compensation amounts.

- Details of other fringe benefits, including:
  - o Cars
  - o Life insurance
  - o Disability insurance
  - o Convention costs
  - o Other special benefits provided to doctors
- If there were any related party transactions, they were identified and quantified in dollars. These included family members of Company X who were on the practice payroll, and loans or lease agreements between the corporation and Company X. Complete details were required for any arrangements like this.
- Curriculum vitae on doctors.
- Listing of all employees, including the physicians, indicating job title, employment dates, hours worked per week, compensation, and any special designations.
- Collection ratio for the practice, at least for 2006, and, if available for 2008. This is the ratio of cash collections to charges for the period.
- One-page summary description of the practice, including:
  - o General data such as practice location, doctors' names and years of each in practice
  - o Hospitals served
  - o Brief description of patient base
  - o Specialties offered by the physicians
  - o Office hours
  - o Any "extra mile" services offered to patients
  - o Statement as to why the practice is successful
- Estimated value of expendable supplies inventory at the end of July 2008, including major equipment.
- Corporate federal and state income tax returns for the last three to five years, prepared by corporate CPA.
- Corporate financial statements for the last three to five years, prepared by corporate CPA or internally.
- Self-employed schedule from each physician's tax return for the last three to five years, if applicable.

- Copies of malpractice and business insurance coverage and premium billings. Specifically, we would review the 2006 and 2008 annual premium amounts, the periods covered and payment dates.
- Current fee schedule for the ophthalmology practice. Noted on the schedule was the date of the last fee adjustment and whether or not Company X is participating for Medicare purposes (i.e., accept assignment).
- Any marketing information regarding the practice, including brochures, patient education materials, advertisements, etc.
- A notation as to the most typical referral sources for the practice.
- Information regarding any HMO or PPO programs in which Company X is participating, including basic information describing the program, the payment mechanism, whether or not capitation payments are received, and an estimate of the percentage of the practice gross volume composed of this type of patients.
- Patient data (estimated if necessary):
    - Number of new patients per month
    - Total number of patients involved in the practice
    - Number of major procedures per month for 2008
    - Patient demographics, including percentage of practice composed of Medicare patients and any further breakdown as to age groups that could be provided
    - Number of patients seen on a daily, weekly or monthly basis by each doctor, on average.
    - Percentage of the practice patient base that is covered by insurance.

## TERMS AND CONDITIONS

1. All financial statements, tax returns, operation information and other data relative to the corporation have been provided by management and have been accepted without further verification.
2. The valuation reported is for the purpose defined in the scope of this assignment, and such valuation may not be relevant for any other purpose. No further use of the reported valuation is authorized, anticipated or intended.
3. All estimates of value are presented as an expression of the valuator's judgment, based upon the facts and date obtained from all sources used in developing the valuation.
4. The values presented are stated before any taxes related to the transfer of any ownership interest.

5. There is no guarantee that the estimated value reported would be realized, in cash or otherwise, if the shares of the corporation valued were offered for public sale, either now or at any future date.

6. We (the valuation consulting firm) have no financial interest in the corporation of Company X.

7. The fee for this valuation service was not contingent upon the value reported.

8. This evaluation follows the protocol and the by-laws of the Institute of Business Appraiser's, Inc.

## DEFINITION OF FAIR MARKET VALUE

Fair market value is defined as "the price at which the property would change hands between a willing buyer and a willing seller when the former is not under any compulsion to buy and the latter is not under any compulsion to sell, both parties having reasonable knowledge of the relevant facts."

(Revenue Ruling 59-60)

"Often an appraiser will find wide differences of opinion as to the fair market value of a particular stock. In resolving such differences, he should maintain a reasonable attitude in recognition of the fact that valuation is not an exact science. A sound valuation will be based upon all the relevant facts, but the elements of common sense, informed judgment and reasonableness must enter into the process of weighting those facts and determining their aggregate significance. The fair market value of specific shares of stock will vary as general economic conditions change from "normal" to "boom" or "depression," that is, according to the degree of optimism or pessimism with which to investing public regards the future at the required date of appraisal."

(Revenue Ruling 59-60)

## SUMMARY OF GENERAL INFORMATION

### Professional Corporation

The Company X has established an ophthalmological specialty at 1 Main Street, ________, _____, and has been incorporated under a personal services corporation, Form 1120 U.S. Corporate Income Tax Return, since October 10, 1972. They are currently on a fiscal year ending October 31, but it has been the recommendation of this consultant, acknowledged by the CPA and the administrator Mr. G, that they will move to a year-end fiscal year. It should also be clearly noted that the optical shop, utilized within the walls of Company X, is valued as a part of the overall value of said corporation at a value of $998,207. This appraiser, as directed, reviewed and broke out the optical shop showing an approximate value of $285,000 for the optical-only value. This would leave, if the optical shop is not acquired, an overall clinic value of $713,585. This is per the direction of Mr. G and the two owners, Dr. X and Dr. Y.

The intent of this practice appraisal valuation is to present a fair and equitable price for the potential buy-in of the Optometrist and the Ophthalmologist currently employed under a standard employment arrangement by said corporation. It is the intent that this evaluation must be affordable and must be something that is fair and equitable under the guise of the Internal Revenue Service and The Institute of Business Appraisers, Inc. We will state that a personal request came from both Dr. ZZ and Dr. Z to break out the optical shop as they may or may not be interested in that value and the buy-in of that entity. Therefore, they have options to buy-in to the overall corporation or to buy-in to the clinic only or to buy-in to the optical only. They will have this variety per the request of the corporation and the individual employed physicians.

May we state clearly that after appropriate analysis and research in this state, at the corporation site, that this appraiser is keenly aware that previous owners have bought in and have bought out of this corporation using a totally different mathematical formula. It is a formula that has a derivative and a percentage based on accounts receivable and values therein. Though we recognize that for previous employees and previous owners, this has been a probable and appropriate mathematical model that will use different criteria than we would use, and though we use that as appropriate intelligence, we did not solely use part of or partially develop my appraisal using that knowledge or that model.

The fee structure of this subject corporation appears to be below average in the market place in the state. We have also assessed its participation status with Medicare and found that to be reasonably valid with limited exposure to fraud and abuse. We believe this corporation is widely respected primarily due to the development of Dr. Y, Dr. X, Dr. H and Dr. W. These are the ones who have made this practice successful, and we believe with limited other competition in the area that with the development of the ambulatory surgery center, this corporation will succeed on an ongoing basis. This corporation has developed an outstanding newsletter and patient education brochure and is engaged in very professional refractive marketing. We give due credit for this to the existing owners, Dr. X and Dr. Y, along with their administrator and CPA, Mr. G. These very devoted ophthalmologists, as owners in this practice, have applied so many appropriate, prosperous business strategies that their development has been almost totally insulated from reimbursement shifts and the depletion of market share and patient volume. Dr. X and Dr. Y and the other senior staff should be credited for many years of service in the development of their fine reputation that appears to be unmatched in the competitive marketplace with other ophthalmic practices.

## Staffing

We were vividly impressed with the primary team leaders of each of the locations, optical shop, clinic, lab, business office and refractive marketing. The FTE (full time equivalency) appears to be exactly where it should be relative to this size of corporation. It could be argued that this corporation employs tenured, long-term employees, therefore, creating a higher payroll allocable amount to the overall budget. Since turnover is the number one problem in ophthalmological practices today, we will suffer the higher payroll for the tenure and loyalty of this fine staff. The main office of this corporation, located again on 1 Main Street, is at a high volume one-way street that gives them high visibility and a beautiful, excellent building location. It is our understanding that the real estate is owned under a separate partnership, and again we will reiterate, this appraisal does not include any real estate values or any denotations to the future ASC. It refers only to clinic and optical shop. It should be clearly noted that this corporation has built a fine reputation mainly from the development of almost thirty years at this ophthalmic location. We give due appropriate credit to the senior Ophthalmologists who have provided this lovely, aesthetically pleasing location on Main Street. We will indicate to you, with their diversification to refractive, their fine profitability and options on the optical shop, development of an ambulatory surgery center, that they are focused on great future success with those diversification and business strategies. We do not see this corporation moving downward, only upward, from an economic and reputation standpoint. All who are involved in this fine corporation should be credited and should be very pleased to know there is real value in this ophthalmological location.

## VALUATION CONSIDERATIONS

In order to reach a sound, reasonable conclusion as to the fair market value of a corporation, we generally analyze and give consideration to the following factors, as they are provided for our review:

1. The status of the corporation as of the valuation date.
2. The size of the medical corporation being valued.
3. The history of the practice, the ophthalmology specialty and the management of the corporation.
4. The financial condition of the corporation from a historical perspective, as of the valuation date.
5. The estimated net asset value of the corporation as of the valuation date.
6. Operating results of the professional corporation for a representative period of time, with particular regard to the estimated earnings of the corporation before payment of physician compensation, discretionary fringe benefits and income taxes.
7. The valuation has not been completed with any regard to tangible assets.
8. It is anticipated that any buyer of said corporation would be purchasing 100% of stock in the professional corporation, if applicable.
9. Although consideration has been heavily reviewed in terms of the impact of RBRVS and the future of Medicare, it should be noted that we feel the full impact of Medicare RBRVS has already been felt by Company X. Therefore, we have not factored in any loss to RBRVS for the future.

   The weights have been appropriately distributed, as the valuator would purposefully do with any ophthalmology practice, outlining three formats for valuation as follows:

   a. Excess earnings

b. Gross receipts

c. Excess future earnings discounted cash flow

## RESULTS OF VALUATION STUDY

We have prepared this valuation study at the request of the management and the corporation. The purpose of this valuation is to assist management of this corporation in determining a price that might be asked for the sale of the corporation to other certified ophthalmologists, hospitals and/or other entities. The results of this valuation study are not intended for any other purpose.

As a result of the valuation study, we estimate that as of July 31, 2008, the approximate fair market value of Company X is $998,207, inclusive of the optical shop. We have determined that the optical shop value is a part of the $998,207 and is valued at approximately $284,622. Furthermore, we have determined the approximate value of the clinic alone would be $713,585. The reader of this document must understand it is my strongest recommendation that the two owners, Dr. X and Dr. Y, keep and collect the accounts receivable. In other words, we have not included the accounts receivable as a tangible asset in this appraisal. It is our clear assumption that the existing owners will own and collect and maintain the accounts receivable.

***ESTIMATED FAIR MARKET VALUE COMPANY X: $998,207.00***
***(In total and inclusive of the optical shop)***

## METHOD OF VALUATION

The valuation of a professional medical corporation must consider both the tangible "hard" assets of the practice and the intangible goodwill value associated with it. The valuation of net tangible assets focuses on the estimated fair market values of the corporation's tangible assets, less the known financial liabilities of the corporation. The valuation of goodwill is considered more subjective and generally involves application of some multiplier to either practice gross receipts and/or practice earnings available to owners. Below is a more detailed description of the methodology used to arrive at the estimated values for both tangible assets and intangible assets of the professional corporation.

## ESTIMATED VALUE OF NET TANGIBLE ASSETS

The corporation maintains its books and records using the cash method of accounting. Although this is the typical method of accounting used by private medical practices, it does not adequately reflect the total tangible assets or financial liabilities of the corporation in accordance with generally accepted accounting principles. Even financial statements prepared in accordance with generally accepted accounting principles do not fairly reflect the market values of the corporation's tangible assets. Therefore, it was necessary to adjust the cash basis financial statements of the corporation that had been compiled by management.

We did not audit, review or compile any financial statements for the corporation. The financial statements provided by management were analyzed and adjustments were made to reflect estimated market values for tangible assets and financial liabilities, and to recognize unrecorded assets and liabilities of the corporation. The most significant adjustments to the corporation financial information are summarized below.

| | | | |
|---|---|---|---|
| 1. | Accounts receivable, to clearly remain with sellers or owners and to be collected only by them: | $ | -0- |
| 2. | Medical supply/Optical inventory (2 weeks supply):$ 15,000.00 | | |
| 3. | Optical Inventory (estimated 950 frames @ $27 wholesale): | $ | 25,650.00 |
| 4. | Prepaid expenses: | $ | -0- |
| 5. | Equipment less accumulated depreciation (under Schedule L 10B $136,829.00 market replacement costs shows a 52% weighted value): | $ | 71,151.00 |
| 6. | Accounts payable (1 day): | $ | 2,500.00 |
| 7. | Notes/Loans (any notes will be paid at closing): | | -0- |
| 8. | Current liabilities (plan payable): | $ | 400.00 |
| 9. | Accrued salaries, wages and taxes: | $ | -0- |

## ESTIMATED VALUE OF NET TANGIBLE ASSETS
## Company X as of July 31, 2008

***(Note: No real estate and/or building value is included in this valuation.)***

| | | |
|---|---|---|
| **CURRENT ASSETS** | | |
| Cash | $ | -0- |
| Accounts receivable, less uncollectible | $ | -0- |
| Medical supply | $ | 15,000.00 |
| Optical Shop (Inventory) | $ | 26,650.00 |
| Prepaid expense | $ | -0- |
| **ESTIMATED TOTAL CURRENT ASSETS** | **$** | **41,650.00** |
| **EQUIPMENT** | | |
| Estimated fair market value | $ | 71,151.00 |
| ***ESTIMATED TOTAL TANGIBLE ASSETS*** | ***$*** | ***112,801.00*** |

**CURRENT LIABILITIES**

| | |
|---|---|
| Accounts Payable (2 weeks) | $ 2,500.00 |
| Notes/Loans (amortized thru 12/31/07) | $ -0- |
| Liabilities | $ 400.00 |
| Accrued salaries and taxes | $ -0- |
| **ESTIMATED TOTAL CURRENT LIABILITIES $** | **$ 2,900.00** |

**ESTIMATED VALUE OF NET TANGIBLE ASSETS**

| | |
|---|---|
| Estimated total tangible assets | $ 112,801.00 |
| Estimated total liabilities | $ 2,900.00 |
| ***ESTIMATED VALUE OF NET TANGIBLE ASSETS*** | ***$ 109,901.00*** |

*All assets acquired after July 31, 2008, will not be a part of the appraisal, but may be added at Dr. X's and Dr. Y's discretion to bring the appraisal up to date.

NOTE:

1. Numerous vendors were contacted in terms of developing this tangible asset position and to develop the estimated value of net tangible assets. There were management reports that indicated a complete physical asset inventory. This data was used, along with phone contacts, to evaluate the final determination on net tangible "hard" assets.
2. It should be further noted that this valuator will recommend the accounts receivable be removed from this tangible asset position and be denoted as –0–. The existing owners should maintain and collect the accounts receivable. An individual buyer will not be buying into accounts receivable.
3. The optical shop is included in the overall value of this corporation, Company X, but also separated at the end of this report.

## ESTIMATED VALUE OF INTANGIBLE ASSETS (GOODWILL)

The valuation of goodwill and intangible assets has been determined by combining the results of three different approaches. The first approach is the excess earnings method. This method estimates the value of goodwill from a comparison of net earnings for the subject practice to other ophthalmology practices, both nationally and within the same geographic area.

The second approach is the gross receipts method. This approach is more general in nature, focusing only on the gross receipts of the practice and the ophthalmology specialty. The value of goodwill is determined as a percentage factor of the annual gross receipts of the subject practice.

The third approach is the excess future earnings, discounted cash flow method. This approach measures the goodwill value of the practice by estimating the net present value of the future benefits of the above average earnings stream of the practice.

The following pages provide a more detailed description of all three methods and the indicated goodwill values produced by each approach.

## ESTIMATED NORMAL EARNINGS FOR OPHTHALMOLOGISTS

In determining the estimated goodwill value of a medical practice, the valuator normally reviews the gross receipts and net earnings of the subject practice in relation to other comparable practices of the same specialty. Presuming the data is reasonably available, the medical practice will be measured against other practices within the same geographic area as the subject practice.

Due to licensing requirements, medical practices are typically sold, in whole or partial interests, to physician buyers. There are other potential buyers of medical practices, such as hospital corporations, but these transactions are much less frequent. The perceived goodwill value of a medical practice to a physician buyer normally relates to the earnings of the subject practice in comparison to what the physician buyer might expect to earn if he/she established a practice of his/her own in the same specialty and in the same market area. To the extent the subject practice generates earnings above the norm, and if the physician buyer can reasonably expect to benefit in future years from retention of that above average earnings stream, the practice is perceived as having goodwill value.

In determining the estimated goodwill value of Company X, it was necessary to develop the estimated normal earnings for an ophthalmologist in private practice, within the same region of the country. Several resources were used in development of the normal earnings estimate. Primary emphasis was placed on survey results published recently in industry periodicals, including *Medical Economics* and *Ocular Surgery News*, and through The Appraiser' clients, MGMA data and the Robert Morris Foundation. The valuator also drew on other sources of information available.

After considering the information available that pertained to ophthalmology practices it is this valuator's judgment that normal earning for ophthalmologists in this particular geographic area would approximate $220,000 per year. This is before payments for physician retirement and income taxes.

***ESTIMATED NORMAL EARNINGS FOR OPHTHALMOLOGISTS: $220,000.00***

***$220,000 × 2 owners for a weighted line item estimation of $440,000 = the average earnings of ophthalmology***

## ESTIMATED GOODWILL VALUE—EXCESS EARNINGS METHOD

This method estimates the value of goodwill based on a comparison of the earnings for the subject practice to other ophthalmology practices, both nationally and within the same geographic area. This corporation is a closely held private corporation. The earnings available to the owner(s) of this type of corporation are usually defined as earnings before owners' salary, discretionary fringe benefits, retirement plan contribution and corporation income taxes. The earnings to the owner were analyzed for the past three to five years based on tax returns that have been filed with the Internal Revenue Service.

This approach involves development of weighted average earnings for the practice. The most recent years' earnings are assigned higher weighting, based on the assumption that they more fairly represent future earnings expectations. Quite often, the valuator will weight the most recent year with a value of three, the next most recent year at a value of two, and the earliest year with a value of one. However, in certain circumstances heavier weighting of the most recent years might be deemed more appropriate. For this corporation, a normal approach to the weighted average level of earnings available to owner was believed reasonable, and was used.

The estimated level of normal earnings for an ophthalmology practice was determined by the use of comparable statistics for other ophthalmology practices and clients. Reported earnings within the geographic area and national earnings data were considered. The estimated normal earnings were compared to the weighted average earnings available to the owner over the past three to five years to determine the excess earnings of the subject practice. The excess earnings were then capitalized. A capitalization rate of .20 was believed reasonable for this practice situation. The result is the estimated goodwill value of the practice using the excess earnings method. This method is summarized on the following page.

## ESTIMATED GOODWILL VALUE—EXCESS EARNINGS METHOD

Excess Earnings Method—Average Ophthalmologist solo $220,000 times two (2) owners; break-even point equals $440,000. This only applies to the excess earnings salaries to Dr. Y and Dr. X, but this does not refer to Dr. H.

| Calendar Year Ended | Earnings (comp. & ordinary income) | Weight | Weighted |
|---|---|---|---|
| (a) 2008 | $491,500 | 40.00% | $196,600 |
| (b) 2007 | $617,916 | 40.00% | $247,166 |
| (c) 2006 | $619,418 | 20.00% | $123,884 |
| Weighted average earnings to owner: | | 100% | $567,650 |
| Weighted earnings to owner(s): | | | $567,650 |

| | |
|---|---|
| Less the average earnings for ophthalmologist: | - 440,000 |
| Excess earnings of practice: | $127,650 |
| Capitalization rate (divided by): | .20 |
| ***Estimated goodwill value, rounded:*** | ***$638,250*** |

NOTE:

1. Earnings to the owner are based on U.S. Corporation Income Tax Returns.
2. No real estate or building is included in this valuation.

## ESTIMATED GOODWILL VALUE—GROSS RECEIPTS METHOD

This method estimates the goodwill value of a medical practice by applying a valuation factor to the gross receipts generated by the practice. The factor value varies depending upon the type of practice under consideration. Practices with high patient retention and return rates tend to have higher factor values than surgical specialties and referral based medical subspecialties.

Ophthalmology practices are normally viewed as favorable practices to sell and buy because they have continuing patients, as in primary care, plus high-fee surgical procedures. In recent years, the factor value has approached 100%, which produced a goodwill value of one year's gross receipts. However, Medicare reduced the allowable fees for cataract operations, and Congress enacted the Medicare Physician Payment Reform and Resource based Relative Value Studies (RBRVS). Nonetheless, it is the belief of this valuator this will have no current effect on the corporation, as the five-year cycle is basically completed. The result has been a decline in the valuation factor for ophthalmology practices to a range of approximately 20% to 35%. For the purpose of this method, I will use 21%.

Mature practices with long-established records of superior earnings, especially in a competitive market, tend to command higher valuation factors. Newer practices, those with average results, and those in areas with little or no real competition, will typically have lower valuation factors. In consideration of the age of the subject practice, office locations, earnings' performance, and area competition, a gross receipt factor of 20% is deemed reasonable for purposes of this valuation.

The projected gross receipts for the calendar year ending October 31, 2008 is believed to be the most appropriate amount for this approach. The 2008 gross receipts require adjustment to reflect the estimated impact of the additional associate. Reference is made to the adjusted earnings recap for further details regarding this adjustment.

| | |
|---|---|
| 2008 Gross receipts through 12/31/08: | $ 3,920,000 |
| *We are validating that this will be "on track" for the year 2008 gross receipts | |
| Less imputed salaries: (1 MD & 1 OD): | - 300,000 |
| Adjusted gross receipts: | $ 3,620,000 |
| Overhead pro forma: | -3,493,333 |
| Net profitability gross receipts: | $ 126,667 |
| Owner compensation: | $ 500,000 |
| The net profitability with an add back of owner compensation must be achieved to develop any earnings before interest and taxation. | |
| EBIT (Earnings Before Interest and Taxes): | $ 626,667 |
| Capitalization Rate: | 1.5 |
| ***Estimated goodwill value gross receipts method rounded:*** | ***$ 940,001*** |

*This appraisal does include the optical shop.

## EXCESS FUTURE EARNINGS DISCOUNTED CASH FLOW METHOD

This method estimates the goodwill value of a medical practice based on the net present value of the anticipated excess future earnings stream of the practice. Future earnings are estimated on the basis of either current practice earnings, or a detailed forecast for future periods. A discount rate is selected based on current risk-free rates of return, plus a factor for the perception of risk involved in either achieving the forecasted results or retaining the existing income stream.

There was no detailed forecast prepared to project the anticipated future earnings stream for this practice. Therefore, the adjusted earnings for the calendar year ended July 31, 2008, were used for this approach. A discount rate of 18% over a five-year period was determined to be a reasonable rate of return and capital recovery period that would be expected by an investor. This is based on current mid-term rates for risk-free investment, and a premium for the perceived risk of retaining the current income stream in the ophthalmology field. This rate and term also approximate the typical financing rate and repayment term a physician might expect to obtain if the financing was obtained from a commercial bank.

| | | |
|---|---|---|
| Net earnings 2008 | | |
| (profitability after all overhead including owner compensation): | $ | 627,000 |
| Reimbursement (10%): | | - 62,700 |
| Adjusted Future: | $ | 564,300 |
| IBBOSTEN, risk and reward method (21.4%): | | - 120,760 |
| Adjusted Cash Flow Projection: | $ | 443,540 |
| Future Earnings Discounted (18%): | | 79,837 |
| True Adjusted Future Earnings: | $ | 363,703 |
| Capitalization Rate (40%): | × | .40 |
| ***Estimated Goodwill Value, Rounded:*** | ***$*** | ***909,258*** |

## ESTIMATED GOODWILL VALUE – SUMMARY

Each of the methods used to estimate the value of goodwill has support, and should be considered in determining the total estimated value for the goodwill of the practice. However, all methods are not necessarily equally appropriate in all circumstances. Therefore, the values indicated by each approach have been weighted based on the perceived applicability to the practice. More weight has been given to the excess future earnings methodology, because it takes into account more of the factors specifically related to the practice of the corporation in ophthalmology today. The future earnings method has employed a 70% value each in the evaluation of the cash flow and profitability of Company X.

| Valuation Method Goodwill Value | | Weight | Weighted Value | |
|---|---|---|---|---|
| Excess earnings | $ 638,250 × | .10 | $ | 63,825 |
| Gross receipts | $ 940,001 × | .20 | $ | 188,000 |
| *Excess future earnings | $ 909,258 × | .70 | $ | 636,481 |
| ***ESTIMATED GOODWILL VALUE, ROUNDED:*** | | 100% | ***$*** | ***888,306*** |

*Excess future earnings is the preferred methodology.

| | | |
|---|---|---|
| Asset position: | $ | 109,901 |
| Goodwill Value: | $ | 888,306 |
| ***ESTIMATED GOODWILL VALUE, ROUNDED:*** | ***$*** | ***998,207*** |

NOTE:

1. Due to the impact of PPMCs using historical multiplier, we have used the excess future earnings as the most predominant methodology.

2. The optical shop revenue is included in overall value.

3. No real estate is included in this appraisal.

## ESTIMATED VALUE OF THE PROFESSIONAL CORPORATION COMPANY X

The fair market value of the corporation is believed to be equal to the sum of the values of the corporation's net tangible and intangible assets. Following is a summary of the indicated values for both net tangible and intangible assets for the corporation of Company X.

| | |
|---|---|
| Estimated net tangible asset value: | $ 109,901 |
| Estimated goodwill value: | $ 888,306 |
| ***TOTAL ESTIMATED VALUE: COMPANY X*** | ***$ 998,207*** |

We have been requested by the owners, the employees and the administrator of this said corporation to value the optical shop. We have evaluated the optical shop at the following levels:

a.) In terms of the overall value compared to a volume assessment of 31% optical volume, one would then calculate 31% of $998,207 to come up with an optical shop value of $309,444.

b.) It is the true computation of future earnings to value 60% of the cash flow of the optical as being a valuable and appropriate tool. This methodology means if the overall optical shop cash flow is $433,000 projected to the corporation, then other optical shops are valued at 60% of cash flow for one year. Therefore, 60% of $433,000 produces a value of $259,800.

c.) It is our belief that both of these applications are appropriate. Both standard evaluation methodology and true percentage of overall value of said corporation. Therefore, we have equally weighted, at 50% weight, each of the values: $309,444 and $259,800, to come up with an optical shop weighted value of $284,622. If this is the true value, then the clinic would be valued at $713,585 or a combined value, both clinic and optical, of $998,207.

NOTE:

1. The amount of data comprised indicated to this valuator that heavy utilization of excess future earnings methodology should be used.

2. We have noted no impact from real estate within the appraisal.

3. The optical shop has been valued separately at an overall weighted value, as noted above, of $284,622.

4. We have dealt with a total estimated value that is a reflection of the most conservative approach to ophthalmology through the next 5 years, through the year 2013, using the excess future earnings discounted cash flow methodology.

5. A weighted factor of 20% capitalization has been denoted in various categories for impacts of true capitalization with considerations to cataract surgery and RBRVS.

6. It is assumed that an outside buyer would purchase 100% of the overall corporate value, excluding real estate, at $998,207.

7. It has been the election of this valuator to put heavy emphasis on the excess future earnings discounted cash flow methodology for goodwill valuation. It should be clearly understood by the corporation that valuations could be performed in a myriad of fashions. Even though this evaluator has selected to utilize heavy weights on excess future earnings methodology, the valuation could be skewed based on another valuator's determination.

8. The decrease in Medicare reimbursement (RBRVS) has been evaluated. It was determined that this decrease has had relatively no impact on this corporation's location.

9. Distribution Value of Total Ownership Compensation: It is appropriate for this evaluator to look at the affordability of a buy-in to a corporation that has an approximate value of a million dollars. We have assessed the opportunity of the MD and/or OD, both or individually, to buy-in to said corporation. We have determined that if $720,000 is the overall basic owner compensation, at the very least a three-owner combination would drive a $240,000 per-owner compensation package. A four-owner compensation package would, at the very basic equal distribution, drive a $180,000 base incentive owner compensation, without any determination made of increased volume, better reimbursement, lowering of overhead or increased net profitability.

10. We would further assess that if you would normalize the true earnings of this corporation, the available earnings on a normalized earnings basis is at $900,000. If you base this on a four-owner combination, then each of the owners would obviously approximate a base salary, without incentive, of $225,000. Is it prudent, at an average buy-in, of trying buy-in to $998,207 at a level of 25%, economically? It has been my determination that the monies owed for 25% buy-in would approximate $249,552. That $249,552, paid over seven years without consideration to interest, only on a static amount of principal, would over seven years average $35,650. We must determine an interest add-on, but still would allow a junior partner to buy-in at the prescribed above value level and still maintain a base compensation of at least $190,000. That indicates economic prudence and appropriate value to said valuation.

## ADJUSTED EARNINGS RECAP

The valuation has not included an adjusted recap earnings position. It is felt by this valuator that it would not have present or historical value, because of the limited amount of excess depreciation, compensation and other related benefits. Due to the debt service, which is limited on the corporation, we felt the typical items that would be included in the adjustment were not present and the computations not completed. Typical items for adjustment to reported earnings were not calculated, but encompass the following: earner's compensation, excess depreciation, business taxes, associate compensations, associate benefits, associate receipts, rent waiver, shared expenses, and loss of any disposal situations. Without question, a very conservative approach was taken to the valuation, and the associate's impact for 2008 was clearly denoted.

## INCOME TAX CONSIDERATIONS

It should be very clearly noted to the management of the corporation that the income tax considerations were not addressed during this evaluation. Not only were the reports unavailable for conclusions to be drawn, but also, time was limited under this engagement. It is my impression that the income tax consideration issues can effectively be dealt with separately.

The market comparable information obtained for purposes of the valuation is also generally presented on a pre-tax basis. Most medical industry business journals present practice financial information as gross profit before owners' salaries, retirement contributions and income taxes. Accordingly, the comparison of earnings of the subject practices to other comparable practices has been done on a pre-tax basis. The resultant determination of excess earnings for the subject practices has been capitalized at a rate that is believed reasonable for application to pre-tax earnings for medical practices and ambulatory surgery centers.

In this valuator's opinion, after-tax earnings would be totally inappropriate. Accordingly, no further consideration of income taxes is deemed necessary.

## ITEMS NOT CONSIDERED IN THIS VALUATION

1. Tax Impact to Physician – Tax planning to structure any potential sale has not been considered.

2. Continuity of Physician and Ownership – The valuation assumes there would be no significant change in the current physician(s) participating in the practice. The validity of this assumption is contingent upon the physician(s) remaining with the practice or, if not, the corporation's ability to retain patients and records.

3. New Shareholder's Contribution to Growth – Newer physician shareholders usually contribute to practice growth, both before and after obtaining ownership. It can be very difficult, and, in many cases impractical, to determine whether practice growth is attributable to the goodwill of the practice or to the presence of any particular physician of physicians. This issue is more related to finalizing the transfer price between specific individual buyers and sellers than it is to the determination of the value of the professional corporation as an operating entity. Accordingly, no adjustments to value have been considered to recognize this factor.

4. Value of Real Estate – No real estate or property was involved in the completion of this valuation.

5. Appraised Value of Equipment – Management elected not to have a formal appraisal of the office and ophthalmic equipment owned by the corporation. The equipment has a cost basis, less a fair market value, in today's market place. By contacting numerous vendors, conducting interviews with the CPA organization and evaluating other ophthalmic practices, a price was derived. The estimated value for equipment was arrived at by many specific methods, based on estimated market devaluation from original cost. The variance between the estimated equipment value herein and the result of an actual equipment appraisal is unknown. It was the subjectivity of the valuator to be able to make the final determination as to the estimated fair market value of equipment.

## BUY-IN ILLUSTRATIONS

The following caveats should be in place as an understanding from the corporation, management, president and CPA organization that certain exceptions have been made to this valuation report in a buy-in consideration.

1. If an individual or outside entity wants to buy-in to the entire corporation of Company X at 100%, it would be at a value of $998,207.

2. There is no real estate configured and/or figured in this appraisal.

2. The optical shop is a derivative of $998,207 and has been valued at $284,622 giving an ultimate clinic value of approximately $713,585.

## NOTES AND ASSUMPTIONS

1. Plan for buy-in to take place at the end of the associated contract term.
2. This will require new employment contracts that specify the following:
   a.) Compensation for each year during the buy-in term
   b.) Net production target for each year during the buy-in term
   c.) Definition of net production same as in the associate contract
   d.) Incentive compensation percentage based on that production in excess of target specified
   e.) Term for contract same as buy-in term
   f.) Termination to the party with reasonable notice
3. We anticipate a full 100% buy-out of this corporation, Company X, at $998,207 which would be completed in a cash settlement at closing.
4. The sale of 100% interest in the corporation's stock is anticipated.
5. The corporation will buy stock back at a predetermined rate if the relationship goes sour prior to completion of buy-in terms.
6. A plan to draft a buy/sell agreement at time of buy-in to protect both physicians in the event of death, long-term disability, retirement or other termination from practice.
   a.) Establish corporate practice value using the same method to determine buy-in.
   b.) Fix value of predetermined amount for new corporation until expiration of buy-in period. After buy-in period, value the new corporation following the same method used to determine the buy-in.
   c.) In the event of a buy-out, assign a value of total buy-out amounts of stock. Pay out rest and departing shareholder's equity and practice value as deferred compensation up to a five-year term.
   d.) As long as there are only two shareholders, give the corporation the right to dissolve and buy out any departing partner, except in the incidence of retirement, death or long-term disability. Consider insurance funding for both death and disability buy-outs.
7. The fees collected are cash receipts resulting from fees as determined by the valuator.
8. Fee growth has been anticipated at a value years one (1) through five (5) at 9% and in years six (6) through seven (7) at 12%. This, again, encompasses the determination of RBRVS and future ophthalmological reduced reimbursement. Growth rate of those percentages is nominal and competitive with the market place.

9. Application to buy-in represents salary differential dollars that would be left in the corporation for Dr. Y and Dr. X to take as additional compensation.

10. Net earnings estimates compensation the employee would be able to take out before taxes. This would also be the taxable compensation amount for the new employee.

11. Interest factor used at 10%, when applicable, is current prime rate. All payments include the interest factors.

12. Payments assumed monthly salary differential payout.

13. As to timing, it is assumed the employee would buy-in at the end of the current employment contract term.

14. We anticipate a 25% buy-in by an employed physician; therefore, 25% of the correlated $998,207 would approximate a 25% buy-in at a level, without interest, which needs to be configured at $249,552.

15. No down payment is expected at closing for the purchase of the corporation by an outside entity.

16. In no way has this valuator attempted to analyze the impact of the safe harbors as noted in the December 1995, 1996, 1997 and 1998 Federal Registers. It is recommended that the appropriate health care legal counsel review the safe harbor conditions. It is our understanding, as of April 15, 1992, however, that a physician-to-physician sale under one corporate umbrella is still permitted. However, we would still suggest legal counsel review and analysis.

17. The initial salary of the employed physician has been computed at a rate commensurate with the market place of ophthalmology.

## UTILIZED AS A BUY-IN ILLUSTRATION AND/OR AFTER THE BUY-IN COMPLETED—FUTURE INCOME AND EXPENSE ALLOCATION

After the buy-in terms have been completed, future income collected in the practice will be allocated totally in the ratio of net charges generated by each physician for the full corporate fiscal year. Net charges are simply gross, less discounts and write-offs.

Expenses will be separated into three components:

1. Those that are direct, i.e. professional liability premiums, individual meeting expenses, individual dues, contributions to retirement accounts on behalf of the physicians, and all other chargeable expenses. The latter are generally optional expenses paid through the corporation for tax purposes, including automobile allowances, disability and medical insurance premiums, individual entertainment, and promotion, etc.

2. The balance of expenses will be separated into two components; each containing one-half of the remaining operating expenses. The first half of these expenses will be allocated equally under the presumption that, approximately, this portion of the expenses is fixed and thus should be borne by each doctor regardless of the level of his/her productivity.

3. The other half of the remaining operating expenses will be allocated in the same ratio as income collected for the first fiscal year.

The compensation payable to the physician will be based on the excess of their allocable income collections, over their share of the allocable expenses, as outlined above. To protect corporation cash needs, the corporation will have the right to retain up to 5% of the excess annual income collections and overall annual operating expenses, excluding physician compensation and retirement contributions.

## PROFESSIONAL CORPORATION

### Company X

Key Points for Dr. X and Dr. Y to consider with the employee ophthalmologist if he/she is the individual who is looking for buy-in:

1. Option to Terminate—If the associate is not meeting production targets, or if the arrangement is not working out, you have the option to terminate.

2. Trial Period—Production targets designed to recover cost of the associate, including fringes.

3. Associate Period—The amount applied to the buy-in is profit to the corporation, available to the owner.

4. Stock Purchase—Requires no down payment from associate, but the corporation will gain in an economic sense from the deferred compensation program and apply to buy-in. This is a non-deductible investment by associate, which will be paid by after-tax dollars, as intended for the buy-in.

5. Profit Motive—The intent is to cover the cost of the associate from the buy-in before any incentive payments are made to the associate. Incentive percentage is designed protectively, so as not to exceed the profit ratio available for Dr. X and Dr. Y.

6. Taxation to Dr. X and Dr. Y—All monies received will be compensation, taxable as ordinary income. To this extent, payments will be deductible by the corporation. If laws change, it should qualify for capital gains treatment.

7. Return to Dr. X and Dr. Y—In proposed form, the combination employment and buy-in projects a real return for the professional corporation, only to Dr. X and Dr. Y, of approximately $1,000,000.

## NOTES FOR ASSOCIATE EMPLOYMENT CONTRACT

1. Specify term—approximately 24 months.

2. Specify compensation for each period.

3. Spell out production targets.

4. Explain incentive compensation.

5. Covenant not to compete needed and the radius therein.

6. Identify fringes to be paid for the associate.

7. Specify what costs will be paid regarding meetings, conventions, seminars and other professional travel.

8. Termination at will, by either party, with reasonable notice requested.

## POSSIBLE APPROACHES TO VALUATION OF PATIENT ACCOUNTS IN A BUY-SELL AGREEMENT

If a physician leaves the practice and takes patients to a new practice location, you need a mechanism to value the accounts. You might consider valuing the individual accounts for this purpose based on the following formula:

(Sum of last three years' billings) × .33 × .65 = account value

Alternatively, you could take a simpler approach. Applying the following formula, using the prior twelve months' collections attributed to the departing physician:

(Sum of last 12 months' collections) × .65 = value of accounts

Either formula would roughly approximate the goodwill value assigned to patient accounts in the practice valuation that was just completed. To the extent that a physician takes patient accounts upon departure from the practice, the value of those accounts would offset any amount the physician would be due under the buy-out arrangement.

## IDEAS REGARDING BUY-SELL

1. Comparable Buy-In and Buy-Out Values—Generally, the method used to value a practice for purposes of a buy-in should also be applied to determine the value for a buy-out. The value will change over time, but the method for arriving at the value can be agreed upon at this time. You may elect to change the methodology at a later date based on changing values for ophthalmology practices and/or surgery centers in the market place.

2. Appraisals—You can elect to have the practice appraised each time that a buy-in/ buy-out occurs. This may be the fairest way to handle both types of transactions. However, in the long run, many physicians will choose a basic formula and review the formula for reasonable notice every few years.

3. Corporation Ownership—Since you are practicing within a professional corporation, individual physicians will only own their respective shares of stock. All assets and liabilities will belong to the corporation. No one will actually own any specific assets, such as cash, accounts receivable or equipment. Rather, you will own a percentage of the corporation that owns these specific assets.

You do not have to decide who gets specific assets or assumes certain liabilities unless you are liquidating the corporation. You only deal with those specific asset values if, in the event of a buy-out, a shareholder is receiving certain corporation assets instead of cash. In those instances, you merely need to define how those assets will be valued. For instance, accounts receivable will probably be valued based on age. Equipment would probably be valued by a qualified appraiser, and supplies would likely be valued at replacement cost.

4. Patient Charts and Records—You need to decide how you will determine the right to patient charts and records. It would seem logical to assign these records based on which physician has been delivering the services to specific patients. This should be readily available from your computer system. The fact that a particular patient was a patient of the practice prior to the buy-in becomes irrelevant. It is presumed that the buy-in will have included that particular patient in the determination of the practice value. It is my understanding that there are many state medical societies that feel the protocol of purchasing patient charts and records is, at the very least, considered an unethical practice. One should check with state medical and/or licensing boards to determine the ethics behind a patient chart or records purchase.

5. Valuation of Patients Taken—If a physician leaves the practice and takes patients to a new practice location, you need a mechanism to value the accounts. You might consider putting a value on the individual accounts for this purpose, based on a formula that would roughly approximate the goodwill value assigned to patient accounts in the practice valuation that you will receive. To the extent that a physician takes patient accounts upon departure from the practice, the value of those accounts would offset any amount the physician would be due under the buy-out arrangement.

6. Income Sharing—You need to decide how you will distribute practice income to all shareholders. Normally, I recommend that this will be an appendix to the buy/sell agreement, because the income division plan tends to change with changes within this specific practice. This will help you avoid more frequent revisions to your buy/sell agreement document. There are about as many ways to divide practice income as there are corporations. However, patient accounts, buy/sell agreements and the possible income sharing formula for shareholders denote any anticipated viewpoint on the subjects.

7. Retirement Plan—You will probably maintain the corporation profit sharing plan. Ordinarily, expenses with corporation employees are considered a part of the overhead. The contribution on behalf of each physician owner is considered a part of their total compensation. This is because each owner's retirement contribution is, typically, a direct function of their compensation.

8. Buy-Out Price Under Special Conditions—You might decide that it would be appropriate to change the buy-out price under certain circumstances. Some professional corporations will discount the buy-out price if the buy-out is taking place as a result of circumstances that are not considered discreditable to the corporation. The thought here is that the discreditable acts damage corporate goodwill. Examples would be bankruptcy, conviction of felony, or expulsion from the state or national medical association. This is a philosophical question I recommend you discuss.

9. Unpaid Buy-In Liability—If a partner leaves the corporation during his/her buy-in period, the unpaid liability for the buy-in would be deducted from the buy-out value. In essence, he/she has a liability here which is not fully paid.

10. Buy-Out Terms—I believe that the buy-out terms should generally favor the corporation. This is based on the premise that continuing the medical corporation is your primary objective. Therefore, the buy-out terms should be comfortable for the corporation.

    Sample terms might be as follows:

    a.) Stock Purchase—Buy the departing shareholder's stock based on the accrual basis book value of the corporation, excluding goodwill. Pay approximately one-half of the shareholder's prorated portion of the accrual based book value upon departure. Finance the balance of the payment for stock over a five- (5) to seven- (7) year term.

    b.) Goodwill Value—Pay out goodwill value as deferred compensation. This makes the payments fully deductible by the corporation, which lessens the actual cash cost for the buy-out. The payments would be fully taxable to the departing shareholder as ordinary income.

    c.) Interest Factor—The deferred portion of the stock buy-out and deferred compensation amount should include a reasonable rate of interest. I normally recommend using prime rate, adjustable, no less frequently than annually. However, you might fix the buy-out interest rate at 10%.

    d.) Annual Payment Limit—Payments for a buy-out to a departing shareholder should not put the corporation in a severe cash flow situation. You might consider limiting the corporation's annual liability for buy-out to a percentage of corporate net earnings, before owners' compensation and fringe benefits. A limitation of 15% net earnings would probably be sufficient.

11. Option to Liquidate—You need to consider whether or not you want to put yourselves in a position of being required to buy-out the other shareholder(s). If there are only two shareholders involved, you should retain the option to liquidate the corporation.

12. Death or Disability—Payment for death or disability normally is similar to pay-out for a departing shareholder who is not taking any business or assets at the time of the departure.

13. Life or Disability Insurance—A decision needs to be made regarding the purchase of life insurance or disability buy-out insurance. Term life insurance is a fairly inexpensive way to fund a buy-out in the event of a death. Disability buy-out coverage is more expensive, but is worth considering. Many professional corporations are beginning to purchase disability buy-out policies for at least a portion of the estimated buy-out liability for each partner.

Note: A buy/sell life or disability insurance program is a necessity under the risk formula for any stockholder in any medical corporation. One must put in place an appropriate cross purchase program.

14. Disability Term—The decision needs to be made regarding at what point a shareholder will be permanently disabled. The term is normally nine (9) to twelve (12) months. A decision also should be made as to how long the corporation will pay a person's salary during disability. Typically, this is no more than six (6) months. The shareholders are expected to purchase personal disability coverage beyond the six- (6) month period. If a decision is made to fund disability payments beyond the six- (6) month period, those additional payments are deductible from any subsequent buy-out if the buy-out is later triggered by permanent disability.
15. Grounds for Expulsion—You might want to consider under what circumstances the shareholder could be expelled from the corporation.
16. Fringe Benefits—You need to decide what fringe benefits of the corporation will be paid for by the corporation, and which benefits will be paid by the individual physician. Benefits paid by the corporation will become a part of the corporation overhead. To the extent they are paid by the individual physician, they will not be an issue. You may decide to pay certain discretionary fringes within the corporation for tax purposes.
17. Vacations—These items are typically dealt with within employee contracts. You may decide to have this part of your buy/sell arrangement if all other compensation issues are dealt with in the buy/sell.
18. Disputes—It is recommended that disputes under the buy/sell agreement be submitted to binding arbitration.
19. Limitation to Owners—The buy/sell agreement might be in place to identify what can and cannot be done without a certain percentage vote. Examples might be major purchases of equipment, incurring debts, admission of new shareholders, execution of new lease agreements, etc.
20. Restricted Stock—The stock in the corporation should be restricted as to transfer. You do not want any shareholder to have the ability to transfer stock to a third party.

## SUMMARY

I realize this is a long list of items for you to consider. The more complete your buy/sell agreement is, the better your chances are of avoiding misunderstandings in the future. The buy/sell agreement that you execute at this time will not be with you forever, but it should be a step in the right direction. Again, the critical issue, unfortunately, is a buy/sell arrangement that deals with an unforeseen disability. It is an absolute priority that any medical corporation sets in motion this type of buy/sell arrangement.

## REAL ESTATE

I want to make it very clear that this appraiser has not appraised the real estate. It is not a part of this appraisal. It should be, if appropriate, under the partnership that a local real estate appraiser conducts the real estate appraisal for purposes only, if desired by the partnership, of sale in the local market. Real estate is not included in this appraisal.

## OVERALL SUMMARY AND CONSIDERATIONS

I would like to thank Mr. G, Dr. X and Dr. Y, for the opportunity to complete this practice appraisal project. It should be understood that although assumptions were made, an exhaustive amount of time was spent to make this valuation as fair and equitable as possible. This has been gleaned clearly through the philosophy of the excess future earnings method. This approach takes into consideration all possible parameters of the health care environment, inclusive of Medicare RBRVS, and other inherent changes within the health care environment in this state. Furthermore, we have investigated and reviewed in a cursory fashion the safe harbors exhibited in the July 1991, June 1992, and December 1993, 1994, 1995, 1996, 1997 and 1998 *Federal Registers*. Again, it is anticipated that legal council will be sought and advice given by the appropriate attorneys in regard to this key issue.

This appraisal has been completed, analytically, under the auspices and the guidelines of The Institute of Business Appraisers, Inc. This appraisal has been completed to the best ability of The Appraiser to arrive at a fair market value for an extremely successful corporation. I attempted to give you an appraisal value using various methodologies, encompassing the theory behind the practice valuation in terms of tangible assets and estimated goodwill. I have addressed options in terms of buy-in protocol for an outside entity. However, it is the belief of this valuator that any prudent buyer would want to purchase 100% of said corporation and would also consider a buy-out of the real estate and building location, after that evaluation is completed. This evaluation is for the professional corporation only and does not include real estate and/or building in the state or geographic area.

Again, this valuation was completed as a reflection of the valuation date of July 31, 2008. It is my best estimate as to the profitability of the corporation's assets and the appropriate goodwill through the three methodologies utilized, separate from the actual physical asset position of the corporation.

The "I" word, i.e., intangible value, has struck fear into many physicians and/or hospitals over the last few years. Physicians buying into a practice are sometimes reluctant, even hostile, to admitting an intangible value exists. Many advisors to physicians, including lawyers, accountants and consultants, will often advise them not to pay for the intangible value when buying into a practice. Most often, those advisors are sincere in the advice they offer, however, they are also often not aware of what is actually happening in the marketplace today. Without question, in today's health care environment, the movement toward ownership by hospitals and other entities, as well as buy-ins by employee doctors of single partner owned corporations, are not only clearly in vogue, but the way of the world for the next four to five years. The conditions of the health care environment have created the continued search for every potential advantage for both buyer and seller. The individuals reading this report should understand that normal earnings are a difficult thing to calculate. Even though we have referenced many statements utilized, inclusive of the Robert Morris Associates' annual statement studies for SIC code 8011 (services for doctors), again, with all data that has been reviewed, the numbers could be skewed plus or minus 3%-5%.

It is the assumption from the perspective of the seller that any cash position and/or pension would remain with the seller; also remaining with seller would be the accounts receivable with those appropriate monies withdrawn upon closing. Therefore, this valuator has not considered a robust position of cash and/or any determination of pension, as it is clearly assumed this would remain with the seller. Furthermore, any basic liabilities that are on the books for the seller would, of course, be removed before a buyer would acquire this corporation.

To reiterate, it is my clear belief that any valuator, though learned in his/her respective field, could evaluate this corporation at a different level. It is my hope that this corporation will review the content of this valuation with the knowledge that I have worked in the health care industry for over twenty (20) years as a sole owner of my corporation, along with working with the Blue Cross Blue Shield plans and Medicare during the previous seven (7) years, for a total of twenty-seven (27) years in the health care industry, which has enlightened me. I have worked with numerous appraisals, especially in ophthalmology, and have the knowledge base to give you a clear opinion of the fair market value of this corporation. It should be so noted that this evaluator has critically taken into consideration through July 31, 2008, the impact of the Physician Practice Management Companies (PPMCs) of ophthalmology. We believe it is appropriate and prudent to bring up to date the financial perspectives of said corporation. It is also imperative that the most current multiples utilized in the nation by the PPMCs for ophthalmology are noted, taken into consideration and validated through July 2008.

This evaluation is only for the professional corporation and optical shop, and does not include building and/or real estate. It is this valuator's intent that this document should be read as a personal and confidential document and utilized for the sole use of a buy-in/buy-out by an employee of outside entity, to be shared with no one outside the boundaries of the corporation. It has been my approach to deal with this in a fair and equitable manner, and understanding again, the limitations of time and expense to correlate this full practice valuation under the guidance of The Institute of Business Appraisers, Inc. We feel this is the best attempt to arrive at a fair and marketable practice valuation. The tax ramifications need to be appropriately reviewed and the conditions, therein, need to be satisfactory for both buyer and seller. Again, we would like to thank Dr. X, Dr. Y and Mr. G for their support and assistance in completing this appraisal of Company X. Please contact us directly with any questions from the report. We hope the practice appraisal fulfilled your expectations. We look forward to speaking with you after you have had an opportunity to digest this report so that we can begin the appropriate negotiations and buy-in of said corporation by your existing employed Ophthalmologist and/or Optometrist.

## Chapter 8

# Refractive Earnings & Market Share Calculation (REAMS CALC)

*A simple test makes it easy to see which elements of your refractive surgery practice are on a par with the most successful practices, and which are not.*

Surviving in today's increasingly competitive marketplace necessitates setting appropriate fees, tracking economic factors such as net income and market share, and carefully managing overhead.

Knowing your practice's numbers is very important. But seeing where your practice stands in relationship to other successful practices can be even more valuable; it can help you pinpoint areas in which your practice may be in need of attention. (Having too many employees, for example, can be a major financial burden, yet the problem may be invisible if you have nothing against which to compare your current staffing arrangement.)

Unfortunately, few clear-cut benchmarks for a successful refractive surgery practice have been available. And the average successful refractive surgeon is far too busy to do an extensive economic comparison to other practices.

## Setting the Standard

We at Health Care Economics have generated a set of benchmarks representative of a successful refractive practice in today's market. To do this, we surveyed more than 100 practices to determine what financial and marketing numbers a healthy, thriving refractive practice usually displays.

Many of the practices we chose to survey were taken from our own pool of clients; others were selected by asking outside companies, such as laser manufacturers, which practices were performing the most procedures. Our primary criterion was that the practice had to be making at least 90% of its income from refractive surgery.

The result of our survey is a measurement tool we call the **Retained Earnings and Market Share Calculations** or **REAMS-CALC**. Using this tool makes it easy to compare your practice's financial information to that of a successful refractive practice.

You may be skeptical about comparing your practice to a hypothetical ideal practice. Many doctors feel their practices are unique, justifying significant financial differences uncovered by REAMS-CALC. In our experience, however, refractive practices are universally competitive; thus, these numbers apply to most successful practices. The cost of doing business, for instance, tends to be consistent from practice to practice. Lasers have similar access fees, and refractive surgery is primarily a cash business.

Admittedly, factors such as rent may vary. However we've found fairly consistent percentages and rations among successful practices, regardless of size, marketplace, physical location or other factors.

In short, we have assembled a reliable series of benchmarks for a refractive practice. If your figures are significantly different, focusing your attention on the area or areas that aren't up to the REAMS-CALC standards should make a real difference in the economic viability of your practice.

## Getting the Whole Picture

In this chapter, we provide a simplified version of the REAMS-CALC tool that you can use in your own practice. Key categories you will need to compare include:

- Fee structure
- Net income
- Accounts receivable
- Overhead (broken down by category)
- Staffing (full-time equivalent employees per physician)
- Asset/income ratios
- Marketing budget (percentage of gross income)
- Market share penetration analysis (number of likely patients available in your market.)

As you can see, the REAMS-CALC tool is designed to provide a complete measurement of the economic status of a refractive practice.

## Data Required

1. Non-Compete/Confidentiality Agreement with a signature required by both parties.
2. List of Competitors within a radius of 100 miles around the central office must be considered.
3. One (1) to two (2) years of Profit & Loss Statements, Balance Sheets and Income Statements or Financials
4. Expected exit time frame, value determination and/or appraisal and the exit strategy.
5. Current fee schedule considering refractive pricing, unilateral and bilateral.
6. Staffing complement, salaries, date of hire and last merit consideration.
7. Accounts receivable or financial policies therein.
8. Professional team (including your CPA, consultant, attorney) location and phone numbers, website or e-mail address.
9. Marketing budget and business plan relative to television, radio, print or other media.
10. Any additional, critical information that the individual refractive practice would like include.

On the following page is a graphical explanation of the Refractive Earnings and Market Share Calculation or REAMS calculation.

## Sample Practice Retained Earnings and Market Share Calculation

| Item | Benchmark | Actual | Difference | Areas of Concern |
|---|---|---|---|---|
| Net Income (percent of gross) | 61%- 64% | $2,003,594 (40% of gross) | Only about 2/3 of benchmark | ✓ |
| Expenses (percent of gross) | 36-39% | $2,448,837 (49% of gross) | 10% to 13% higher than benchmark | ✓ |
| Total global bilateral fee | $3,750.00 | $3,400 | Only 90% of the benchmark fee | ✓ |
| Accounts Receivable | 10% | $262,000 (5%) | ½ the benchmark amount—good! | |
| Marketing Budget | 5% of revenue | 6.7% of revenue | 1.7% higher than benchmark | ✓ |
| Ratio of assets to liabilities | 5:1 | 14:1 | Much higher than the benchmark | |
| High-volume competitors in the area | Enough to leave 3,500 potential eyes per year | 2 competitors performing about 1,750 procedures per year | Plenty of potential patients remain in the market | |
| OVERHEAD | | | | |
| Marketing | 5% | $287,100 (5.8%) | A little higher than the benchmark | |
| Uniform, travel, CME | 0.5% | $38,700 (0.8%) | 1½ times the benchmark | ✓ |
| Legal and Accounting | 0.5% | $64,000 (1.3%) | Almost 3 times the benchmark | ✓ |
| Medical Supplies | 2% | $163,800 (3.3%) | Almost double the benchmark | ✓ |
| Laser Access Royalty | 8% (Volume driven) | $615,442 (12%) | 1½ times the benchmark | ✓ |
| Rent | 4% | $165,057 (3.3%) | Below the benchmark | |
| Salaries | 9% | $381,815 (7.7%) | Only 85% of the benchmark | ✓ |
| Professional fees (OD, etc.) | 2% | $198,976 (4%) | Twice the benchmark | ✓ |
| General miscellaneous Expenses | 5-10% | $247,500 (5%) | Within acceptable range | |
| Total | 36%-41% | 48% | 7-12% higher than the benchmark | ✓ |
| STAFF | | | | |
| Average Cost | $37,104 | $30,920 | Only 83% of benchmark amount | ✓ |
| FTEs per MD | 4 clinical<br>2 surgery<br>2 business | 8 clinical<br>2 surgery<br>2 business | More clinical staff than benchmark (Doctor preference) | ? |
| FTEs per OD | 2 clinical<br>2 business | 2 clinical<br>2 business | Same as benchmark | |

## Using the REAMS-CALC Chart

On page 14, you is a sample of the REAMS-CALC chart filled out by a hypothetical doctor. Some key information about this doctor:

- His yearly gross income is approximately $4,950,000.
- He practices in a city of about 1 million people.
- He performs approximately 2,900 procedures per year.

Here are some comments to help clarify the meaning of some of the categories and how the numbers are calculated.

**Net Income and Expenses**—Having too high a level of expenses is a common problem, particularly in the areas of marketing, staffing and fees paid for laser access.

**Global Fee Structure**—The most successful refractive practices don't try to compete by lowering prices. Instead, they sell their services on the basis of their skill and experience, as well as the quality of care and follow-up they offer. If your fees are lower than the benchmark, you should consider raising them.

**Accounts Receivable**—If your accountant uses the accrual system, this number may be misleading; the accrual system allows some existing debt to be omitted from this number. If your accountant uses the cash system, your accounts receivable figure should be representative of your true current situation.

**Laser Access Royalty**—This figure will vary, depending on volume. However, 8% is a good average figure, and if your percentage is significantly higher, you should look for the reasons.

**General Miscellaneous Expenses**—Usually an additional 5%-10% is added for expenses such as insurance, janitorial, depreciation and laundry.

**Full-time Equivalency**—When calculating the number of full-time equivalent staff, don't count any staff members twice. (An MD and an OD should each be represented by two business staff members, for example.)

**Ratio of Assets to Liabilities**—Generally, anything higher than 5 to 1 should be considered excellent. However, a lower ratio may simply indicate a major recent purchase. If your ratio is lower, consider it a cause for investigation, not alarm.

**High-Volume Competitors**—To complete these calculations, you will need to take into account the number of people living in your market area.

In our experience, a current population of one million people represents (on average) about 35,000 eyes likely to be potential candidates for refractive surgery. Most successful surgeons perform about 3,500 procedures per year. (Obviously, you should adjust these numbers to reflect your particular market and practice, if possible.)

By determining the number of procedures your high-volume competitors are performing, you can determine an approximate number of potential eyes that are available to you. Our sample doctor works in a city of one million people, with the potential mentioned above. Because he has only two competitors, who perform about 1,750 procedures a year, he should have an ample supply of potential patients.

## Calculating the REAMS-CALC

Filling out the REAMS-CALC on the following page will take a bit of time and effort, but we think you will find it to be very worthwhile. After all, the first step in making things better is finding out there's room for improvement. Using the sample on page 114 as a template, enter the figures from your own practice to determine the areas of concern.

### Retained Earnings and Market Share Calculation Chart

| Item | Benchmark | Actual | Difference | Areas of Concern |
|---|---|---|---|---|
| Net Income (percent of gross) | 61%- 64% | | | |
| Expenses (percent of gross) | 36-39% | | | |
| Total global bilateral fee | $3,750.00 | | | |
| Accounts Receivable | 10% | | | |
| Marketing Budget | 5% of revenue | | | |
| Ratio of assets to liabilities | 5:1 | | | |
| High-volume competitors in the area | Enough to leave 3,500 potential eyes per year | | | |
| OVERHEAD | | | | |
| Marketing | 5% | | | |
| Uniform, travel, CME | 0.5% | | | |
| Legal and Accounting | 0.5% | | | |
| Medical Supplies | 2% | | | |
| Laser Access Royalty | 8% (Volume driven) | | | |
| Rent | 4% | | | |
| Salaries | 9% | | | |
| Professional fees (OD, etc.) | 2% | | | |
| General miscellaneous Expenses | 5-10% | | | |
| Total | 36%-41% | | | |
| Average Cost | $37,104 | | | |
| FTEs per MD | 4 clinical<br>2 surgery<br>2 business | | | |
| FTEs per OD | 2 clinical<br>2 business | | | |

Chapter 9

# Managed Care Contracts: Reading Between the Lines

*Contracts with these entities are negotiable, and physicians should exercise caution in evaluating every program that comes across their desks.*

Health care in the United States today has taken a high profile. It is difficult to pick up any newspaper or magazine without reference to the problems of health care, especially rising costs. Exactly what is wrong with health care in the United States? There are millions of uninsured. Health care costs continue to rise at a pace that far exceeds other areas of the economy. The population is aging. New technology expenses continue to rise. American consumers demands choice and the ability to select their health care providers.

Most of the current literature references "managed care," or one of its many variations, as a potential solution to at least some of the problems in today's world. It is important for you to understand that without physicians, managed care cannot survive. Contracts with managed care entities are negotiable, and as a physician, you should exercise caution when evaluating every program that comes across your desks.

There are numerous concerns and common pitfalls you should scrutinize in managed care contracting, such as:

- You want to make sure the plan is solid and stable.

- You don't want to under- or overestimate the market impact to your practice.
- You don't want to be locked into a contract, even when you want out.
- You might become responsible for services your practice doesn't normally provide, such as drawing blood or providing frames and lenses.
- You may be asked to agree to their rules without seeing them all, then finding out they don't agree with your practice philosophy and patterns.
- You may be required to use referral sources or ancillary providers you don't normally use.
- You may need prior authorization for procedures you normally do in your practice.

## Physician Philosophy

Physicians must understand and be committed to providing quality care in a cost effective environment. As physician, you need to examine your own practice style and philosophy. You should ask and consider:

- Am I truly service oriented?
- Do I practice good communication skills with my patients and colleagues?
- Do I make myself accessible and visible to my patients?
- Do I truly enjoy working in a team environment?

Next, you must assess your interest in quality of care versus financial incentives. Some physicians need to determine where they are in their business and career. The philosophy of the physician who is just beginning a career will be quite different from the physician who is in the middle of a career or the physician who is approaching retirement. The objectives are much different as physicians review managed care and what they hope to accomplish from participation in managed care.

## Administrative Factors

When you are evaluating a managed care contract, there are a number of areas to consider:

1. **Find out who is participating in this particular organization.**

    a. Is your principal hospital a participating hospital?

b. Are the other specialists in your building, or those in your referral network, a part of this plan?

c. Who are the ancillary providers?

d. Is it convenient for your patients to use these other participants?

2. **Find out where the marketing and service areas are for this organization.**

   For example, if they advise you that their 10,000 members live in the fringes, while you are in the center of town, this may not be viable for you. Most organizations are committed to providing access to providers within a 30-minute radius for each patient. In order to determine how their marketing and service areas are related to your practice, calculate the percentage of your current patients who come from that area, and therefore, the resulting impact on your current client base. If you decide to be a participating provider, you will need time for accepting new patients from the organization. If you decide to be non-participating, you must realize the potential of losing some patients, because a managed care organization will direct people to its contracted providers.

3. **Administrative implications**

   Determine how and when you will learn if you are eligible. Consider that in January and July many employers change their coverage options. Often, this means that the managed care entity is unable to keep up with the workflow and provide names of new members prior to the month of eligibility. Find out, if cards have not been issued to their members, how you as a provider will be able to identify the coverage available for a new patient. You may have to make a telephone call to inquire about the eligibility of the patient, or you may have to negotiate with the patient regarding payment for services in lieu of verified eligibility.

   We recommend that once a patient has been identified as a managed care member, you flag the chart in some way noting that his/her co-payment, identification number and effective date of eligibility. Additionally, you may want to consider adding a column to your sign-in sheet indicating the patient's current insurance.

   As a specialist physician within the organization, identify how primary physicians will be notified of your participation so that they have the opportunity to refer patients to you. Identify the method by which the referral will be made. Will the patient carry it to you in writing? Will you be notified by mail? Will someone call your office to advise you that this patient is being referred in the managed care program? These are significant factors since most managed care plans do not allow a patient to self refer to a physician. The referral must be from a primary doctor in the managed care entity. If a patient's medical condition requires treatment over a period of time, how often will you need to secure referral documents to continue treatment? You will find a wide range of circumstances governing treatment decisions with managed care organizations. Some will allow treatment for three months, others for one month, and some will require a new referral document for each visit made to a specialist.

4. **What are the covered/non-covered services?**

At the same time you evaluate the referral program described by the managed care company, find out what services are covered and non-covered. If your practice patterns encompass the use of services the managed care entity has determined to be non-covered, you may want to reconsider your participation in this program. Or at the very least, determine what your options are in terms of securing reimbursement from the patient.

5. **Emergency procedures**

Another area to evaluate in the administrative process is how to handle emergency situations. How do they define "emergency"? For example, would you be permitted to perform emergency surgery for a detached retina without securing prior approval or will you need to detain the patient and contact the organization prior to treatment? These steps are significant to both you as a provider and to the patient, because of their financial implications as well as their quality-of-care implications.

Most managed care companies require pre-certification for surgical procedures. Be sure to determine the methodology required for you to secure this prior authorization. Every entity will have different requirements ranging from a pre-certification number for inpatient surgical procedures only, pre-certification process for all outpatient surgical procedures, or high cost services such as MRIs and CAT Scans.

Again, all of these requirements from the organization will place some administrative burden on your practice. Therefore, you need to address them prior to committing to participation in managed care.

6. **Contractual guidelines**

As you review your contract to make the decision regarding participation in a given program, watch for references to documents that may not be provided. Keep in mind that any document referenced in the contract may be considered a part of the contract. Therefore, you are entitled to see the details of each part. Some of the areas typically referenced, but not included, are the utilization review plan, quality assurance program, standards of care guidelines, and the grievance procedures.

Grievance procedures should benefit both patients and providers. A patient who feels his/her care was questionable must be given a method of challenging this care. Providers who may feel a patient is non-cooperative or disrupting the office must have a method to address the problem. Historically, patients receiving care completely paid for by their insurance company often are more demanding. From the organization's perspective, they want their patient to receive service and quality care. They will monitor providers to ensure that this does take place. You want to make sure your records and documentation support that the managed care patients received equal if not better care (and most certainly not worse care) than private pay patients.

## Capitation Arrangements

1. In the event that a contract provides for capitation to a provider to cover a specific list of services, be certain that the list is complete and coded. Disputes can easily arise if the list is nothing more than a description of the services covered, and such a listing creates substantial room for the plan to interpret the description to suit its own financial interests. Coding prevents this possibility. Further, the contract should state upon which issues of the CPT codebook the list is based and how the plan will handle updating codes from year to year.

   Being certain which services are covered under capitation will also assure you that your evaluation of the value of capitation against projected utilization of capitated services is as accurate as possible.

2. In the event that capitated providers must pay for services rendered by others using their capitation funds, it is imperative that the contract specifically states which party is financially responsible to pay these claims when the contract is terminated and the capitated provider finds that these expenses have exceeded income and/or capitation is inadequate to allow the provider to meet his/her financial obligations. This is not an abstract concern, and the situation currently exists.

3. In the event that a contract provides that capitated services rendered by the capitated provider be paid by that provider regardless of who delivers the service, the provider must realize that in some unique situations this could result in the capitated provider rendering uncompensated services. This potential is exacerbated if the list of capitated services includes a substantial number of expensive procedures that are not performed by the capitated provider.

   The way this works through the payer is that the payer receives claims from providers and checks the services rendered against the list of capitated services. If the service is on that list, the provider is paid out of the capitated physician's future capitation amount and his/her capitation is reduced appropriately.

If the contract provides for such an arrangement, it should specifically describe which services and under what circumstances these services will be reduced from capitation. For example, EKGs might be on the list of capitated services. You might ask, "Under what circumstances is an EKG capitated or payable fee-for-service by the plan?" A typical contract might state that when the EKG is performed as part of an annual wellness physical, it is capitated, but when performed as a result of symptoms, it is payable on a fee-for-service basis by the plan. It should also be noted that if the EKG is payable by the plan on a fee-for service basis when performed as a result of symptoms, the plan should pay whether the service is performed by the capitated physician or a consulting physician, referral facility.

This scenario also raises the importance of ICD-9 coding on claims. When the same CPT code falls under both the capitated list of services and the fee-for-service list of services and the distinction is governed by the reason for the service, the ICD-9 code becomes the driving code.

## Encounter Reports

Encounter Reports are critical to the ability of a plan to set adequate capitation rates. Office staff should be trained thoroughly in how to fill out an Encounter Report. Basically, the Encounter Report should carry only capitated services and should be treated with the same level of respect and accuracy as a HCFA 1500 or a UB 92. In fact, an Encounter Report is a bill to you.

Keeping accurate Encounter Reports allows you the necessary data to negotiate future capitation rates and allows you to keep your own fee-for-service equivalency reports. Keep in mind that when it comes time for the plan to set capitation rates and for you to negotiate and/or act upon your contract, the plan will use your own Encounter Records and resulting fee-for-service equivalency report to support its position. Keeping your own reports will provide you with the same negotiating foundation.

Contracts should state how and when the Encounter Reports will be handled and what should appear on the reports.

If the plan capitates the provider on the basis of age and/or sex, your own fee-for-service equivalency reports should be tracked on the same basis. You may want to support an increase in capitation for just one age/sex cell. Without your own reports on this cell, you have no basis on which to prove your case for increased capitation.

## Coordination of Benefits

Coordination of Benefits (COB), is a critical financial issue for any provider.

Review the contract to determine how the plan will treat COB, who is responsible for COB, and where payments from other plans go.

Pursuing COB on capitated services can do a great deal to improve the value of your capitation under certain types of contracts. For example, you are capitated by Joe's HMO for office visits. The patient, however, has Blue Cross/Blue Shield as primary insurance and Joe's HMO is secondary. You should bill Blue Cross/Blue Shield for the service and apply only the deductible and co-insurance (or non-covered services) to your capitation fund. If the services that are not covered by Blue Cross/Blue Shield are also not covered by Joe's HMO, then you should bill the patient for that service. Your Encounter Report should reflect these adjustments to the initial billed charge.

Most HMO contracts will allow you to keep collections from other insurance. If the contract requires you to turn this money over to the plan, you will need to go into great depth in evaluating the financial impact of such a provision.

In the event that you must pay claims for services rendered by other providers from your capitation funds, COB will be critical to your ability to financially manage your capitation fund. Expert claims adjudication is a necessity in this case.

## Subrogation

Subrogation in this country is extremely difficult and not very productive. However, the contract should carry a provision for which party is responsible for subrogation. It is advisable that the contract makes the plan responsible for this activity and for including your capitated service claims in such action. The contract should also explain which claims will be submitted for subrogation and under what circumstances, as well as how a recovery will be distributed between the plan and the capitated provider. Again, subrogation provisions are most critical when the capitated provider pays for outside services from his/her capitation funds.

## Capitated Reports

Capitated providers are given routine listings of eligible members and capitation reports. It is critical that the contract specifies the frequency and accuracy of these reports and remedies available to the provider when financial damage results from the failure of these reports or the lack of timeliness.

Lack of accuracy in these reports can result in a reduction in appropriate capitation and/or a physician providing capitated services to an ineligible individual.

Further, these contracts provide for retroactive additions and deletions to these lists that directly impact your capitation check. Some plans can retroactively add and delete for a period up to 13 months.

It is suggested that such contracts limit retroactive adjustments to three or four months and that the contract address various scenarios. Contracts that provide for capitated services rendered only by the physician and those which require physicians to pay for outside services from their capitation carry some common concerns in this area. However, contracts that require capitated providers to pay for outside services from their capitation have some unique aspects when addressing these issues.

## Fee-for-Service Equivalency Contracts

The contract should specifically state how frequently the maximum allowable fee schedule will be adjusted and which coding manual will be used from year to year.

## Documents Incorporated by Reference

This is a very real problem. Most managed care contracts refer to documents not provided for review. Remember that any document referenced in a contract may be a part of that contract and when you sign the contract, you agree to abide by or cooperate with the provisions of these documents. No one should sign a contract without having reviewed the provisions of each document mentioned in the contract. These documents typically include:

- Utilization review plans
- Criteria and standards
- Grievance procedures
- Subrogation procedures
- Claims adjudication manuals
- Contracts between the plan and other providers
- Plan specific arbitration procedures, etc.

## Insurance Indemnification, Utilization Review, Restraint of Trade, Breach of Contract, Contract Amendments, Arbitration & Financial Incentives

- Do not sign a contract that places you in the position of indemnifying the plan/IPA/other entity.
- Treat patients using your best medical judgment. This is the priority and should not be influenced by the plan's criteria and standards, utilization review decisions or financial incentives.

- Keep as much distance as possible between yourself and the financial incentives of a plan. The greater the distance, the less likely a lawyer and/or patient can claim that financial incentives influenced your actions and, therefore, harmed the patient.
- Do not sign reciprocal agreements. If you see out-of-state patients, you will be legally liable in that state if you are sued. For instance, PCP in Indiana has reciprocity agreement with a provider in Texas—a provider will go to Texas if sued.

The managed care company offering you a proposal should be able to provide you the utilization rate anticipated for their patient enrollment. By multiplying the number of patient care contracts times the percent of expected utilization, you determine the expected capacity from the contract. Then by comparing the number of patients the contract will obligate you to see to your open slot capacity, you are able to determine if you can handle the increased business generated from this contract.

To determine the relative value computation as it relates to your practice, make three columns in a chart: CPT code, RVU and volume by code. Multiply RVU by volume. Then determine the percentage of the total that each code equals in income. As an example, $66,984 may represent 10% of your volume, but amount to 17% of your income.

## Financial Analysis

While reviewing your managed care contract, pay particular attention to its financial arrangements. If there are claim payments, find out the level of fee schedule that will be used, the turnaround time and any billing practice requirements. Know your resource person at the organization and let him/her know if you are having a reimbursement problem. As with most negotiations, the "squeaky wheel gets the grease."

To determine if managed care is profitable for your particular practice situation, you can use the profit margin analysis outlined in the next chapter. For profit margin analysis, there are three critical areas to determine if the managed care contract is appropriate. Assuming that capitation is the method of payment, you must determine capacity before contracting. As a general rule, you need to be able to accept a minimum of 250 new patients for capitation to prove financially sound. Second, you need to assess your fee-for-service equivalency against the current contract rates offered. Third, you need to evaluate the relative value unit computation.

The first step would be to assess your capacity. In order to determine this, you need to evaluate the number of open slots in the schedule that could be filled by securing new patients through the managed care contract. In a typical ophthalmology practice, you determine the number of open slots in a day and multiply the result by five days in a week and then by 50 weeks in a year to determine the available slots for your practice in a year. With an appropriate mix of postoperative, new patient, established patients and follow-up visits, an ophthalmologist can see three patients in each 15-minute time slot. Again, this will tell you the number of additional patients your practice can see without adding new physicians.

To determine the cost per unit of service, gather data to indicate the total number of patients seen per year. Then divide by the total practice overhead cost to determine the cost per patient per year. Dividing by 12 determines the cost per member per month (PMPM). For a more in depth look at profit margin analysis and how managed care impacts your practice, refer to the next chapter. You will find a detailed explanation and templates to follow that will allow you to calculate figures for your particular practice situation.

## Summary

To determine the economic viability of actual and future contracting, you must be able to arrive at profit margin analysis by knowing the following elements within your practice: Capacity, Overhead, Revenue, and Efficiency (CORE). If you cannot determine these CORE elements for your practice, you cannot position yourself with any consistency. By following the format outlined in this chapter, you will be able to determine the economics, the capacity, and the fee-for-service equivalency of your managed care participation. Once you know your profit margin, your positioning should be apparent.

Besides financial analysis, there are many other components in evaluating a managed care contract. Before you sign a contract, be sure to review the provisions of each document referenced in the contract. You can see from this chapter that from a physician's perspective it is highly important to understand and review the key elements of managed care programs. It is advisable for you to engage an attorney, accountant and health care consultant to assist you with these very complex managed care contract evaluations.

Chapter 10

# Profit Margin Analysis: The Smart Way To Evaluate Managed Care

*This formula was developed to allow the health care provider the opportunity to review critical economic issues when trying to decide whether or not it is appropriate to deal in a managed care, capitated environment.*

Confused about whether to become a provider in a managed care plan? Here is a logical, step-by-step approach that you or your business manager can use to help you determine exactly whether you would benefit by joining the plan. The profit margin analysis for managed care deals with the economic issues for future contracting. This formula was developed to give you the opportunity to review critical economic issues before entering into a managed care, capitated environment. At the end of the chapter, you will find a sample profit margin analysis and a blank one that you can use to analyze your own practice.

You start by determining your costs per unit of service. Being this specific helps you to clearly define what it costs you per member, per annum, and eventually per member per month to pay your practice's overhead. Essentially, you are establishing a break-even point for your practice. Every provider in the market today must understand the cost of doing business per unit or per patient.

Once you have completed this break-even analysis, you will move to Section B, which asks you to add your costs and your expected owner compensation, resulting in your true bottom line. By combining the two, you will know that it costs, for example, $5 to see every patient and to pay owner compensation. This analysis is essential to understanding your real cost of doing business.

Furthermore, you can also analyze existing contracts based on a fee-for-service equivalency so that you can ascertain utilization and capitation rate per unit of service from the members you have seen. Once you have determined your fee-for-service for the patients seen, you combine it with reimbursement to come up with a dollar value for all of those patients under fee-for-service. By comparing the economics of the capitation expectation and the fee-for-service, you gain the knowledge to decide whether or not it is prudent to move forward with a capitated arrangement.

It is evident, in the market today, that many providers feel they must sign all contracts to remain competitive. I believe that rather than engage in contracts that lose you money, you would be better off to increase your market share another way. Taking a closer look, you can achieve further specificity and deeper analysis by breaking down actual overhead by cost centers and then by actual CPT or ICD code. You can be very specific in breaking down overhead by analyzing the code, the associated overhead, and the number of units, which will give you the cost per CPT code. Adding back again the owner compensation will give you an annual break-even per CPT code. To ascertain a monthly profit margin per patient, divide your break-even result per CPT code by twelve.

## What You'll Need

To perform a "Profit Margin Analysis for Managed Care," a set of formulas developed by our firm, you first need to collect the following information:

- Your profit and loss statements.
- Production reports, either for your entire professional corporation or for you personally.
- Post-operative data, which shows the average number of post-operative visits by category of surgery (if possible, use CPT codes for categories).
- The practice's scheduling capacity. The idea is to determine how many open slots you have that could be filled by additional management care plans.

***Use the data you acquire to perform the following calculations.***

### 1. Cost per Member per Month

Take the total number of patients seen in a year and divide by the total practice overhead. The result is what we call the cost per patient per annum (PPPA).

***Example:*** ***10,000 patients ÷ by $500,000 overhead = $50 PPPA***

Remember, you are preparing yourself to compare your costs with capitation amounts offered by managed care plans. So the next step is simply to divide the number by 12 months to determine your cost per member per month (PMPM).

***Example:*** ***$50 PPPA ÷ 12 months = $4.17 PMPM***

## 2. Owner Compensation

Along with covering costs for office overhead, you need to be compensated. Let's say you want to earn 30% over costs. Multiply the PMPM by the percentage of compensation you expect to receive.

***Example:*** ***$4.17 PMPM × .30 = $1.25 Owner Compensation***

## 3. Break-even Profit Margin

This figure will tell you exactly how much money you must make per patient per month to cover costs and earn your desired profit margin. Add the PMPM to the owner compensation amount.

***Example:*** ***$4.17 PMPM + $1.25 = $5.42***

This gives you an idea of what you need to make per patient per month, which is important to know in making intelligent decisions about managed care plans.

## 4. Utilization Rates

Not every plan member is going to use your services, so, in our sample scenario you really need to charge $5.42 per month per user, not per plan beneficiary.

Utilization differs from plan to plan. Certain plan populations may be older or younger, sicker or healthier, more or less likely to see their doctors regularly. Hereditary diseases can have different prevalence from county to county.

To get a more accurate assessment of the number of patients you can expect to gain with the plan, ask the plan to give you an estimate of its utilization rates. Multiply the number of patients enrolled in the plan by the utilization rate to determine the true potential for the plan.

***Example:*** ***5,000 Enrollees × 40% Utilization = 2,000 patients***

***2,000 Patients × $5.42 = $10,840***

Now you have a better idea of the monthly rate you should bid to care for these 5,000 patients: $10,840.

## 5. Practice Capacity

This number is important for several reasons. First, you obviously should not sign onto a plan if you cannot see the patients. Second, knowing your practice capacity gives you an idea of how much room you have to maneuver.

Remember, most of the costs are fixed costs; they stay the same whether you see 10 patients a day or 50 patients a day. If you can see more patients without incurring more costs, it may be worth your while to accept a managed care plan that reimburses you at an even lower level than your $5.42 number. This is a judgment call. You and your staff will work more intensely, but the reimbursements from the extra patients you see will be almost all profit.

Estimate the total number of available 15-minute scheduling slots in a typical day (you may want to take an average over a typical week). Multiply these slots by the number of days you work per week and by the number of weeks you work in a year.

***Example:*** ***4 slots per day × 5 days a week = 20 slots***
***20 slots × 50 weeks per year = 1,000 patient slots per year***

With an appropriate mix of post-op, new and established patients, a physician can see three patients per 15-minute slot. Multiply your available 15-minute slots by three to establish your additional patient capacity.

***Example:*** ***1,000 15-minute slots per year × 3 =***
***3,000 additional patient slots per year***

Now you know that you can accept a managed care plan that would bring in a total of 3,000 extra patients per year without adding physicians or working longer hours. Once you reach full capacity, of course, you can:

- Simply decide not to join any additional managed care panels, or
- Work longer hours or add an associate doctor and continue to join managed care panels.

## Retrospective Studies

You can use as many of these equations to analyze the plans you already accept. Your cost PMPM, desired profit PMPM, revenue and cost for each code, and patient capacity can help you decide whether to continue to accept the same plans. Here's an example of how.

Determine the total number of capitated patients you see per year (not the number of patients enrolled).

***Example:*** ***3,000 enrollees, with 2,000 seen in office***

Now, multiply your capitation rate PMPM by 12 to establish your capitation rate per member per year. Multiply this by the number of members enrolled, and you have established your capitation income from the plan.

***Example:*** ***$5.42 PMPM × 12 months = $65.04 per member per annum***
***$65.04 PMPA × 3,000 = $195,120 capitated income per year***

An interesting exercise is to compare your capitation income figure to the income you might receive from a conventional fee-for-service arrangement. The best way is to compare procedure by procedure, but for a baseline measure, use the intermediate office visit as your fee indicator. Multiply this fee by the number of capitated patients you actually see.

***Example:*** ***$35 intermediate office visit × 2,000 patients seen = $70,000***

If you compare the $70,000 fee-for-service result with your $195,120 capitation income, you will see that it appears to be worth your while to stay with this plan.

To do a truly accurate comparison, you must track the actual number and types of procedures you do on each patient covered by the plan, and then compare your reimbursements.

The volume and revenue for each CPT code will affect the profitability of a given capitation rate. If a plan requires you to perform a large percentage of procedures, which would yield a much higher fee-for-service than the capitation rate you are receiving, it's probably not worthwhile to participate in the plan.

## Conclusion

As a physician, you must get a handle on what it costs to deliver health care. This is the only way to equip yourself to make intelligent choices regarding managed care plans.

Physicians who make intelligent decisions will make managed care work for them. Those who do not, are lot less likely to survive.

The good news is that getting calculating the numbers you need to make the right decision is not difficult. The simple formulas I have described here can help you analyze your current costs, stack them up against the fees you are already receiving, and compare them to managed care proposals.

Next, you will find a Sample Profit Margin Analysis for your review and a Profit Margin Analysis for your practice to use.

## Sample Profit Margin Analysis

**Section I**

**Economic Issues for Future Contracting ***

### A. Determine your cost per unit of service.

Total practice overhead dollars ÷ total number of services per annum =

cost per patient per annum (PPPA)

**$ 1,131,195.00** overhead ÷ actual # of services **12,592** =

**$ 89.83** cost PPPA

Cost per patient per annum ÷ 12 months =

actual cost per member per month (PMPM)

Cost PPPA (from #1) **$ 89.83** ÷ 12 months =

**$ 7.49** PMPM

### B. Compute owner compensation

**$ 7.49** PMPM (from above) × **32 %** owner compensation =

**$ 2.40** owner compensation amount

### C. Compute break-even profit margin

**$ 7.49** PMPM + **$ 2.40** owner compensation amount =

**$ 9.89** break-even profit margin

## Sample Capitation Rate by CPT Procedure

| CPT Code | Historical PMPM | × | Expected Utilization Rate* | = | Minimal PMPM |
|---|---|---|---|---|---|
| 92002 | $9.82 | × | 35% | = | $3.44 |
| 92004 | $10.11 | × | 35% | = | $3.54 |
| 92012 | $9.88 | × | 35% | = | $3.46 |
| 92014 | $9.88 | × | 35% | = | $3.46 |
| 92083 | $9.89 | × | 35% | = | $3.46 |
| 92225 | $9.92 | × | 35% | = | $3.47 |
| 92250 | $8.86 | × | 35% | = | $3.10 |
| 92020 | $9.90 | × | 35% | = | $3.47 |
| 66821 | $9.88 | × | 35% | = | $3.46 |
| 66984 | $9.88 | × | 35% | = | $3.46 |

**Average: $34.32 ÷ 10 = $3.43**

- **Utilization rate for demonstration purposes**

## Capitation Rate by Evaluation and Management (E/M) Procedures

| CPT Code | Historical Based PMPM | × | Utilization Rate* | = | Minimal PMPM |
|---|---|---|---|---|---|
| 99201 | $12.44 | × | 35% | = | $4.35 |
| 99202 | $9.82 | × | 35% | = | $3.44 |
| 99203 | $9.95 | × | 35% | = | $3.48 |
| 99204 | $9.86 | × | 35% | = | $3.45 |
| 99205 | $12.44 | × | 35% | = | $4.35 |
| 99212 | $9.87 | × | 35% | = | $3.45 |
| 99213 | $9.88 | × | 35% | = | $3.46 |
| 99214 | $9.89 | × | 35% | = | $3.46 |
| 99215 | $9.33 | × | 35% | = | $3.27 |
| 99241 | $12.44 | × | 35% | = | $4.35 |
| 99242 | $10.37 | × | 35% | = | $3.63 |
| 99243 | $9.91 | × | 35% | = | $3.47 |
| 99244 | $9.88 | × | 35% | = | $3.46 |
| | | × | | = | |
| | | × | | = | |
| | | × | | = | |
| | | × | | = | |

**Average: $47.62 ÷ 13 = $3.66**

- **Utilization rate for demonstration purposes**

## Profit Margin Analysis for Managed Care

**Section I**
**Economic Issues for Future Contracting**

### A. Determine your cost per unit of service.

Total practice overhead dollars ÷ total number of services per annum =

Cost per patient per annum (PPPA)

$______ Overhead ÷ Actual # of services ____ = $________ cost PPPA

Cost per patient per annum ÷ 12 months =

Actual cost per member per month (PMPM)

Cost PPPA (from #1) $________ ÷ 12 months = $________ PMPM

### B. Compute owner compensation

$______ PMPM (from above) × _____% owner compensation =

$_____ owner compensation amount

### C. Compute break-even profit margin

$_______ PMPM + $________ owner compensation amount =

$_______ break-even profit margin

You now know your break-even point for overhead and owner compensation to achieve the expected profit margin and should therefore not sign any managed care contract for less than the break-even profit margin amount.

## Capitation Rate by CPT Procedures

| CPT Code | Historical PMPM | × | Expected Utilization Rate | = | Minimal PMPM |
|---|---|---|---|---|---|
| | | × | 35% | = | |
| | | × | 35% | = | |
| | | × | 35% | = | |
| | | × | 35% | = | |
| | | × | 35% | = | |
| | | × | 35% | = | |
| | | × | 35% | = | |
| | | × | 35% | = | |
| | | × | 35% | = | |
| | | × | 35% | = | |
| | | × | 35% | = | |
| | | × | 35% | = | |
| | | × | 35% | = | |
| | | × | 35% | = | |
| | | × | 35% | = | |
| | | × | 35% | = | |
| | | × | 35% | = | |
| | | × | 35% | = | |
| | | × | 35% | = | |
| | | × | 35% | = | |
| | | × | 35% | = | |

**Average: $ ÷ = $**

## Capitation Rate by Evaluation and Management (E/M) Procedures

| CPT Code | Historical Based PMPM | × | 35% Utilization Rate | = | Minimal PMPM |
|---|---|---|---|---|---|
| | | × | 35% | = | |
| | | × | 35% | = | |
| | | × | 35% | = | |
| | | × | 35% | = | |
| | | × | 35% | = | |
| | | × | 35% | = | |
| | | × | 35% | = | |
| | | × | 35% | = | |
| | | × | 35% | = | |
| | | × | 35% | = | |
| | | × | 35% | = | |
| | | × | 35% | = | |
| | | × | 35% | = | |
| | | × | 35% | = | |
| | | × | 35% | = | |
| | | × | 35% | = | |
| | | × | 35% | = | |
| | | × | 35% | = | |
| | | × | 35% | = | |
| | | × | 35% | = | |
| | | × | 35% | = | |

**Average: Dollars ÷ Codes = Dollars**

*Figure 4.5 RVU Computation for CPT Procedures*

Chapter

11

# Par/Non-Par Formula

*With Medicare or any other carrier, this formula can be used to assess whether you should participate with that carrier.*

The Participation/Non-Participation (Par/Non-Par) Formula was developed because providers need to be able to access whether they should participate in the Medicare program. Over a number of years, as the participation ranks have grown, this formula has of course been less and less utilized. However, with Medicare or any other carrier, this formula is a good tool for assessing whether you should participate with that carrier.

It is a unique formula for assessment because from an analytical T-Chart viewpoint as it lets you examine all composites of your economic patient base with regard to carriers. It examines the patient base relative to charges, collections, approved amounts, accounts receivable, volume increase and market share penetration.

At the end of this chapter is an actual par/non-par formula for your review. The hope is you will apply this to all contracting today and in the future, as you did with Medicare applications in the past.

The purpose of this computation is to allow you, the provider, to assess not only your price charge base, but to consider how your practice is really doing relative to collection of allowable amounts. You will need to supply the following critical data to complete the formula:

1. A current year-to-date profit and loss statement of revenues and expenses.
2. The last three years' tax returns for your corporation, partnership, limited liability company or sole proprietorship.
3. A list of collection financial data not only by carrier, but by patient, earmarked with the appropriate brackets of 0-30 days, 31-60 days, 61-90 days and more than 90 days.

4. An assessment of your ability to collect money in the front office. This will have to be monitored, usually for a period of six months, to provide accurate collection percentages.

5. You will need to develop a productivity report by CPT code.

6. You will need to develop and review a productivity report by ICD code.

## Market Share Volume Analysis

If you do participate, what market penetration and increase in patient volume can you expect? The converse question also applies. What is the impact to the practice in volume, dollars and loss of patients if you do not participate?

Once you have accessed the items in the list above and have the data needed to complete the Par/Non-Par formula, you will be able to examine more closely every major carrier you deal with and determine the economic impact of participation relative to your geographical access market share. This is a tangible, analytical approach to considering participation versus non-participation in various contracts. It removes the subjectivity from the assessment and makes the decision based more on real economics. Only you can assess other factors, such as the political ramifications of not participating locally in a geographic market with a certain carrier, which also need to be weighed in your decision-making process.

As you review and use this formula, it should help you make a solid economic decision whether to participate with an individual contract, carrier or local independent industrial leader.

Following is a sample of the par/non-par formula which you can use as a template for figures from your own practice.

## Par/Non-Par Formula

| Participating | | Non-Participating | |
|---|---|---|---|
| Charges | 0.00 | Charges | 0.00 |
| Expected Collections | × 75% | Percentage of Collections | × 75% |
| Subtotal | 0.00 | Subtotal | 0.00 |
| Anticipated Approved Amount | × 80% | Limited Charge or Fee Schedule Restriction | × 80% |
| Subtotal of Revenue | 0.00 | Subtotal of Revenue | 0.00 |
| Collection dollars of deductibles and co-pay (non-covered) | +0.00 | Collection of deductibles and co-pay (non-covered) | +0.00 |
| Subtotal of Collection Expectation | 0.00 | Subtotal of Collection Expectation | 0.00 |
| Add back additional volume revenue for participating | +7.5% | Add back additional collections due to non-participating | +5 % |
| Subtotal | 0.00 | Subtotal | 0.00 |
| Subtract expenses related to participation status, systems, staff | -1.5% | Subtract additional expense of non-participation collection | -3% |
| Grand Total | 0.00 | Grand Total | 0.00 |
| Within 5% of each go participating | | Within 5% of each go participating | |

*Figure 5.1 Par/Non-Par Formula Chart*

Chapter 12

# Compliance, Fraud & Abuse

*We are defining fraud as "intentional, deliberate" violations of Medicare rules for "unlawful gain."*

December 10, 1997, *USA Today* reported that $7.6 billion was saved by an "aggressive assault on Medicare fraud, waste and abuse." They removed 3,000 "unsuitable" health care providers from the Medicare rolls. Throughout that year, we read of more cases of increased staffing in the Office of Inspector General (OIG) as well as fines. Our firm had conducted documentation audits all over the country, but we did not find "fraud." We are defining fraud in this case as "intentional, deliberate" violations of Medicare rules for "unlawful gain."

Unlike fraud, abuse can just happen. In fact, improper billing is one example of abuse.

## Seven Examples of Abuse

1. Ignoring the balance billing limits for unassigned claims
2. Charging patients who have assigned their claims to you more than 20% of the Medicare-approved amount
3. Billing patients for charges disallowed by a carrier
4. Violating a participation agreement
5. Billing Medicare at a higher or different rate compared to your "usual charge," generally considered your fee-for-service charge for private patients
6. Billing Medicare when you should be billing another insurer
7. Submitting claims for services that aren't medically necessary—or going

overboard on medically necessary ones by, say, giving a battery of diagnostic tests where only one test is needed

When your carrier reviews claims and suspects abuse, it looks for payment "abnormalities" or unusual patterns of service. It looks for a statistical accumulation of data that makes you different from your peers and suggests you're ignoring standard medical practices or Medicare rules.

The AMA office of the General Counsel has developed a plan which plainly states: "In addition to facilitating high-quality patient care, an appropriately documented medical record serves as a legal document to verify the services provided." At a minimum, AMA suggests that the medical record should be complete and legible, plus the following:

- The documentation for each patient encounter should include: Reason for the encounter and relevant history, physical examination findings, and prior diagnostic test results; assessment, clinical impression or diagnosis; plan for care; and date and legible identity of the observer.
- If not documented, the rationale for ordering diagnostic and other ancillary services should be easily inferred.
- Past and present diagnoses should be accessible to the treating and/or consulting physician.
- Appropriate health risk factors should be identified.
- The patient's progress, response to and changes in treatment, and revision in diagnosis should be documented.
- The CPT and ICD-9 codes reported on the claim should be supported by the documentation in the medical record.

The AMA developed the compliance plan because fraud investigation is a federal priority, and "establishing and maintaining a compliance plan will help physicians in avoiding activities that could be attacked under the fraud and abuse laws."

Even a small office can institute a plan. The AMA identifies seven key elements of an effective compliance plan that can be scaled up or down to fit any practice:

1. **A commitment to compliance** – a statement of conduct that recognizes a set of standards and a plan to ensure that all in the organization understand they must comply with these standards. This is a good faith effort to comply with the laws. To prove fraud, the government has to show willful intent to defraud the government, which would be extremely difficult if this effort is made.
2. **Designation of compliance officer** who holds a high level of responsibility in the organization, and who is trustworthy. In a small office, this may be the physician himself or herself.
3. **Effective training and education programs** so physicians and staff understand their responsibilities under the law.

4. **Auditing and monitoring,** which entails "a regular review of the organization's claim development and submission process from the point where a service for a patient is initiated to the submission of a claim for payment," AMA's plan says. Billing clerks must be aware of the laws and checked on a routine basis—look at claims and documentation, and make sure they're qualified.

5. **Effective lines of communication** concerning compliance within the organization. An employee must feel comfortable telling (the compliance officer) that something is wrong. Two-way communication is needed—the compliance officer must provide information about compliance standards and the results of his/her audits, and the rest of the staff must be able to ask questions and file complaints with confidence that their confidentiality will be maintained, there will be no retaliation, and the . . . complaint will be investigated.

6. **Internal investigation and enforcement** with disciplinary actions.

7. **A process to respond to offenses** and to take corrective actions.

## APPEALS

Because audits do occur, we need to look at the rights of a person who is audited. The appeals process under Medicare has several levels. You must first send your denied claim to your carrier for a re-look or carrier review. The following is an overview of all levels of appeals:

### Level 1 – Carrier Review

You can request a carrier review if you believe a denial was made in error, or if the carrier hasn't approved or denied your claim within 60 days after the claim's receipt. The carrier must use staffers who didn't take part in rejecting the claim the first time around. You must ask for a review within six months of a denial date on the EOB by sending a letter to your carrier.

When sending information to your carrier requesting a review, be sure to include x-rays, test results, medical history, documentation of severity or acute onset, consultation reports, billing forms, referrals, plan of treatment, nurses' notes, and copies of communications between physicians and/or the patient, hospital, carrier and laboratory. After 30 days, with or without additional information, the carrier will begin conducting your review.

You should receive a decision from your carrier about your review within 45 days. You may want to request the information your carrier didn't show you, which is kept in the carrier's file on your case. You are entitled to names, qualifications of any consultants used to decide the claim, all memos of conversations with medical consultants, papers, requests, reports and so forth arising out of the review process. However, you must "request" this information.

### Level 2 – Fair Hearing

To move to the next level of appeal, the claim or claims contested must total $100 or more of controversy. You can't win in a fair hearing by trying to change a Medicare regulation that you think is unfair or illegal. Carriers have no authority to change regulations—they must follow the manual guidelines.

### How to Request a Hearing

Send your carrier Form HCFA-1965 to request a hearing, or write a letter and have it signed by the doctor or a representative. The letter must state that you're dissatisfied with the review determination and you want to appeal further.

### Picking the Right Kind of Hearing

1. A traditional in-person hearing
2. A telephone hearing
3. An on-the-record decision

## Level 3 – Administrative Law Judge Appeals

Physicians have found it well worth their while to pursue these appeals because Administrative Law Judges aren't bound by HCFA's administrative directives to carriers. Administrative Law Judges work for the Social Security Administration instead of HCFA. They tend to have a different perspective on what should or shouldn't be paid by Medicare. The amount in controversy must be at least $500, and no more than 60 days must have elapsed since you received an unfavorable decision under the carrier review for an appeal to an Administrative Law Judge.

### Checklist for Administrative Law Judge Appeal

- ✓ What is eligible for an Administrative Law Judge appeal: Any denied claim for a Part B service valued at $500 or more.
- ✓ How to aggregate claims—yours or with a colleague.
- ✓ When to appeal: Within 60 days of receiving an unfavorable decision from the fair hearing officer. This must be requested in writing.
- ✓ How to request a hearing: Use the Social Security Administration's form ***Request for a Hearing before an Administrative Law Judge*** or a simple letter explaining your request. Use registered mail so you get a receipt acknowledging your request.
- ✓ What the carrier must send to the Administrative Law Judge: Everything about the case.
- ✓ What the request should include: Your name, reason you disagree, evidence and date submitted.
- ✓ Types of hearings: "On-the-record" and in-person.

- ✓ What to bring to the hearing: All evidence.
- ✓ Carriers must begin processing the Administrative Law Judge's decision within 15 days.

## Level 4 – HHS Departmental Appeals Board

If, after going through the Administrative Law Judge process, you lose (or your request for a hearing is dismissed), you have the option of filing a request for review in writing with the Department of Health and Human Services Departmental Appeals Board (DAB). Your request must be filed within 60 days of receiving the Administrative Law Judge decision or dismissal. Your request should include a statement of specific issues or the Administrative Law Judge's findings of fact and conclusions of law with which you disagree. In addition, include other documents or evidence you want the DAB to consider. The Appeals Board will consider the case when:

1. There is an abuse of discretion by the Administrative Law Judge.
2. There is an error of law.
3. The action, findings or conclusions of the Administrative Law Judge aren't supported.
4. There is a broad policy or procedural issue.

If you lose at the Administrative Law Judge and Appeals Board stages, you can file suit in federal district court as long as the amount in controversy is $1,000 or more.

## Medicare Part B Administrative Appeals

The Medicare appeals system is sluggish and not all that it's cracked up to be. First of all, you need to know what can be appealed. For instance, claims that cannot be processed cannot be appealed. However, since the odds are in your favor at the Fair Hearing and Administrative Law Judge levels because they are non-adversarial hearings, you should go fully prepared to prevail.

# MINIMIZE RISK AND CONSEQUENCES

- Understand regulations – Third Party Payer payment rules.

  *Monitor claims processing procedures/policies.*

- Document your records correctly – detailed and legible.

  *"If it's not documented, it didn't happen."*

- Monitor billing profile – Identify changes in frequency or volume of any service.
- Carefully review and follow up on claim denials as well as questions and complaints from patients.

- Cooperate with routine audits and monitor all requests for information for accuracy.
- Beware of Disgruntled Employees – Whistle blower or qui tam lawsuits may entitle employee to receive 25% of gross recovery plus his or her attorney fees.
- Institute a Compliance Program: A well thought out and carefully developed internal compliance program could significantly reduce the risk that you will be subjected to in an audit.

### Compliance Program Goals Are:

- Identify and prevent fraudulent activity.
- Ensure accuracy of billing practices.
- Provide a process for handling wrongdoing.

The Government has promised lighter fines for entities that diligently monitor, find and stop errant activities.

## Elements of a Compliance Program:

- **Written standards of conduct.** The practice must adopt a set of guidelines for everyone in the practice, reflecting the practice's commitment to compliance in general, as well as addressing specific areas of concern for that practice.
- **Designation of compliance officer or committee.** The practice must identify an individual or group of individuals responsible for the operation and monitoring of the compliance program.
- **Education and training for all individuals in the practice.** Programs must be developed to educate individuals about the existence of the compliance program, as well as the rules and regulations with which the practice must comply.
- **Effective mechanism for communication.** The practice must establish a reporting mechanism, through a hot line or other process, for complaints to be communicated to the compliance officer or committee. The compliance officer or committee must also be able to communicate with all individuals in the practice.
- **Internal investigation and disciplinary process.** The practice must develop a process to investigate allegations and, where appropriate, discipline individuals who have acted inappropriately.
- **Periodic auditing and monitoring.** The practice must have a mechanism for performing periodic auditing and monitoring of its operation to assure compliance with applicable rules and regulations.
- **Establishment of response mechanism.** The practice must establish a mechanism to respond to identified problems and establish corrective action to ensure that those problems will not be repeated.

## What Triggers an Investigation or Audit?

All health care providers face the potential of being investigated or audited. Investigations are triggered by information indicating that a provider of care or services is committing fraud or abuse.

**This information comes from:**

- Complaints from patients
- Tips from the provider's employees
- Tips from competitors
- Information gained from investigation of other providers
- Information gained from investigation by other agencies
- Data gathered during the processing of claims

**Types of cases that can result in civil monetary penalties are**:

- Services not medically necessary
- Upcoding
- Gang visits and ping-ponging
- Over-utilization
- Inferior or poor quality care
- Billing for services not rendered
- Altered bills
- Duplicate or false reimbursement
- Claims involving collusion between supplier and recipient
- Claims for non-covered services billed as covered
- Assignment violations

## Your Rights During an Audit

**There are two basic guidelines for responding to audits and investigations:**

1. Cooperate fully with the requests of the investigators, but don't give them more than they specifically request.
2. Settle the matter at the lowest level possible.

**Many auditors do not give you advance notice of their inquiry. They show up at your door and request to see the office manager or the physician(s) being investigated.**

- Verify who they are by carefully checking their identification. Record their names, titles, phone numbers and organization's address.
- If you turn them away, asking for advance notice, they may either produce a subpoena they have with them or return shortly with one.
- Ask whether this is a civil or a criminal investigation.
- Show the auditors to a room where they will be alone and ask them to wait a few moments while you inform your attorney, who may wish to come to the office.

**When the audit actually begins, follow these guidelines:**

- Identify a person within your office to be the contact person for the auditors. All requests, inquiries, etc. should go through this person. This person will remain with the audit team the entire time they are on your premises, so it is impractical to designate the physician.
- Ask that all requests from the auditors be put in writing.
- They will produce a list of what they want to review. The list will include the patient's name and the date of service. They are auditing in response to information about the specific service that was billed to the carrier. Initially, they will be looking at many cases involving that same service.
- They should produce, and you should copy, a patient information release form signed by their beneficiary (your patient).
- Do not give them the entire chart of each patient. Copy only the date of service in question. By giving them the whole chart, you would be providing additional opportunities for them to find fault. Make two copies of each chart page that you provide to the auditors. Lock one up as your record copy of exactly what they received. Date, number and initial each page of this copy, and sign a cover page indicating the audit date and that this copy is an exact duplicate of what was provided to the auditors. This step protects against loss or alteration of the chart between the date of the audit and when the chart may be called as evidence.
- Keep a log of all of their requests.
- Do not allow the auditors to roam the clinic. One disgruntled employee can do a great deal of damage in a very short time.
- Ask when the results of their audit will be available to you.
- Bring your attorney up to date as soon as the auditors leave.

## Risk Prevention Guidelines

Generally, if a healthy client-physician relationship exists, malpractice suits are not likely to occur. Some helpful guidelines to **prevent malpractice** include:

- Staff should perform within the scope of training and education, and should not give advice.
- Comply with state regulations and statutes.
- Keep the office safe and equipment in readiness.
- Practice asepsis.
- Log telephone calls. Return all calls to clients within a reasonable time.
- Avoid treating via telephone.
- Put verbal instructions in writing and give a copy to the client.
- Do not criticize other practitioners.
- Be sure all diagnostic test results are seen and initialed by the physician before filing the slip.
- Explain any appointment delays. Do not keep clients waiting for appointments for more than 20 minutes.
- Select employees carefully and encourage a team approach.
- Keep all matters relating to client care confidential.
- Discuss fees prior to treatment.
- Have employees follow up on missed or canceled appointments and document them.
- Treat all persons equally.
- Never guarantee a cure.
- Continue to grow professionally.
- Secure informed consent as much as possible.
- Listen to clients and always tell the physician when there is a complaint.
- Formally document when (1) withdrawing from a case and (2) discharging a client.
- Carefully follow the Controlled Substances Act—document all information required.
- Keep accurate records.
- Limit practice to scope of training and to a manageable number of clients.

- Call clients at home the day after outpatient surgery to see how they are doing. Document the follow-up in the clients' charts.
- Chart when clients are called with test results.
- Chart all canceled appointments and no-shows.
- Always retain original records or radiographs.
- Have the doctor review files before sending accounts to collection.
- Tell clients how to obtain care on nights and weekends.

## NCQA Guidelines

**Chart Order/Personal Data:**

- Chart order
- Address/Home phone
- Employer/Work phone
- Date of birth
- Marital status
- Emergency contact
- Sex*
- Past medical history*
- Family*
- Social (i.e. alcohol/tobacco)
- Allergies/adverse reactions to medication prominently displayed

**Diagnosis:**

- Diagnosis chart

**Clinical Manifestations:**

- Chief Complaint/Reason for visit
- Physical exam findings
- Current medications
- Patient ID on each page
- Entries legible and dated
- Treatment/Action plan

- Author ID on each entry
- Date of return visit/Follow-up*
- Previous problem follow-up*

**Consultation, Lab and Radiology reports (as appropriate—if ordered):**

- Reports initialed by physician
- Date of review documented
- Follow-up of abnormal diagnostic test results

**Treatment plan and education instruction (as indicated):**

- Medication dosage and schedule
- Home treatment
- Patient education

* *If relevant*

## AMA Guidelines

**Ten Principles of Documenting Patient Records**

1. Physicians should prepare complete and legible medical records.
2. Documentation should include the patient history.
3. Past and present diagnoses should be accessible to the treating and/or consulting physician.
4. Reasons for ancillary services/testing should be recorded.
5. Relevant health risk factors should be identified.
6. The patient's progress should be recorded.
7. A written plan for care should be included.
8. A thought process and the complexity of medical decision-making should be recorded.
9. All entries should be dated and authenticated.
10. CPT/ICD-9 codes should reflect documentation in the medical record.

## Distinguish Between a Consult and a Visit

In general, when billing for a consult versus an office visit, keep in mind who has control of the patient's overall management. A consulting physician may evaluate the patient, order or perform diagnostic services, and start therapeutic service by writing orders. He/she would inform the other physician of the findings and recommendations, and because it is a consult, the patient would be returned to the first physician for any additional treatment and follow-up. If the patient's care is meant to be taken over by the doctor who did the evaluation or ordered diagnostic tests, etc., then the physician's service becomes an office visit, even if it is the patient's first visit.

**Necessary components for a consult include:**

- A request from a physician
- For a stated condition
- For advice or opinion

You will need the UPIN number of the referring physician on your claim forms. Both physicians need to have notes in the patient record regarding the referral. Most practices give their advice or opinion by way of a letter to the referring physician. Copies are retained in the patient chart. In general, this letter is not sufficient documentation for the <u>level</u> of care. Therefore, as required for all Evaluation and Management (E/M) codes, it is necessary for you to document the history, examination and decision making.

**<u>Office/OH Consultation</u>**

| Component | 99241 | 99242 | 99243 | 99244 | 99245 |
|---|---|---|---|---|---|
| History | PF | EPF | D | C | C |
| Examination | PF | EPF | D | C | C |
| Decision-Making | SF | SF | LC | MC | HC |

## Documentation of History

The levels of E/M services are based on four types of history: Problem Focused, Expanded Problem Focused, Detailed and Comprehensive. Each type of history includes some or all of the following elements:

- Chief Complaint (CC)
- History of Present Illness (HPI)
- Review of Systems (ROS)
- Past, Family and/or Social History (PFSH)

## Chief Complaint (CC)

Required for every visit, the chief complaint is the basic reason for the visit. List a concise statement of symptoms, changes and problems.

## History of Present Illness (HPI)

This description, from the first symptom or previous visit to date, includes:

- Location
- Timing
- Quality
- Context
- Severity
- Modifying factors
- Duration
- Associated signs and symptoms

## Review of Systems (ROS)

This includes an inventory of body systems to identify current or previous signs and symptoms. The following systems are recognized:

- Genitourinary
- Ears, Nose, Mouth, Throat
- Gastrointestinal
- Musculoskeletal
- Hematologic/Lymphatic
- Allergic/Immunologic
- Constitutional Symptoms (e.g., fever, weight loss)
- Eyes
- Respiratory
- Neurological
- Psychiatric
- Endocrine
- Cardiovascular
- Integumentary (Skin and/or Breast)

## Past, Family and/or Social History (PFSH)

- Past History (The patient's past experiences with illness, operations, injuries and treatments)
- Family History (a review of medical events in the patient's family, including diseases that may be hereditary or place the patient at risk)
- Social History (an age appropriate review of past and current activities)

The chart below shows the progression of the elements required for each type of history. To qualify for a given type of history, **all three elements in the table must be met.** (A chief complaint is indicated at all levels.)

| Type of History | (HPI) History of Present Illness | (ROS) Review of Systems | (PFSH) Past, Family, and/or Social History |
|---|---|---|---|
| Problem Focused | Brief | N/A | N/A |
| **Expanded Problem Focused** | Brief | Problem Pertinent | N/A |
| **Detailed** | Extended | Extended | Pertinent |
| **Comprehensive** | Extended | Complete | Complete |

## Content and Documentation Requirements

| ***Level of Exam*** | ***Perform and Document:*** |
|---|---|
| **Problem Focused** | One to five elements |
| **Expanded Problem Focused** | At least six elements |
| **Detailed** | At least two elements from each of six areas/systems OR at least twelve elements in two or more areas/ systems |
| **Comprehensive** | At least two elements from each of nine areas/ systems |

## Documenting the Complexity of Medical Decision-Making

The level of E/M services recognizes four types of medical decision-making (straight forward, low complexity, moderate complexity and high complexity). Medical decision-making refers to the complexity of establishing a diagnosis and/or selecting a management option as measured by:

- The number of possible diagnoses and/or the number of management options that must be considered;
- The amount and/or complexity of medical records, diagnostic tests, and/or other information that must be obtained, reviewed and analyzed; and
- The risk of significant complications, morbidity and/or mortality, as well as co-morbidities, associated with the patient's presenting problem(s), the diagnostic procedure(s) and/or the possible management options.

The chart below shows the progression of the elements required for each level of medical decision-making. To qualify for a given type of decision-making, two of the three elements in the table must be either met or exceeded.

| Type of Decision-Making | Number of Diagnoses or Management Options | Amount and/or Complexity of Data To Be Reviewed | Risk of Complications and/or Morbidity or Mortality |
|---|---|---|---|
| Straight Forward | Minimal | Minimal or None | Minimal |
| Low Complexity | Limited | Limited | Low |
| Moderate Complexity | Multiple | Moderate | Moderate |
| High Complexity | Extensive | Extensive | High |

## Number of Diagnoses or Management Options

The number of possible diagnoses and/or the number of management options that must be considered is based on the number and types of problems addressed during the encounter, the complexity of establishing a diagnosis and the management decisions made by the physician.

Generally, decision-making with respect to a diagnosed problem is easier than that for an identified undiagnosed problem. The number and type of diagnostic tests employed may be indicators of the number of possible diagnoses. Problems that are improving or resolving are less complex than those that are worsening or failing to change as expected. The need to seek advice from others is another indicator of complexity of diagnostic or management problems.

Each encounter must have an assessment, clinical impression or diagnosis.

**For an established diagnosis, show if:**

- Improved
- Controlled
- Resolving or resolved

**OR**

- Not Controlled
- Worsening
- Different than expected

**For an undiagnosed problem, show**:

- Differential diagnoses
- Possible/Probable diagnoses
- Ruled out diagnoses

**Management changes that must be recorded include:**

- Patient instructions
- Therapies
- Medications

## Amount and/or Complexity of Data to Be Reviewed

The amount and complexity of data to be reviewed is based on the types of diagnostic testing ordered or reviewed. A decision to obtain and review old medical records and/or obtain history from sources other than the patient increases the amount and complexity of data to be reviewed.

**List all diagnostic tests that are:**

- Ordered
- Planned
- Scheduled
- Performed
- Note request and/or review of old records

## Risk of Significant Complications, Morbidity and/or Mortality

The risk of significant complications, morbidity and/or mortality is based on the risks associated with the presenting problem(s), the diagnostic procedure(s) and the possible management options.

**Comment on factors that increase the complexity of medical care, such as:**

- Underlying diseases
- Other factors
- Risk of complications

**Note surgical or invasive procedures that are:**

- Ordered
- Planned
- Scheduled
- Performed
- Note any referral or service that is on an "urgent" basis

## Summary

Zero tolerance for fraud and abuse should be the goal of every health care provider in maintaining a compliance component.